Evolutionary Dynamics and Sustainable Development

Evolutionary Dynamics and Sustainable Development

A Systems Approach

Norman Clark
SPRU, University of Sussex, UK

Francisco Perez-Trejo
UNITAR, Geneva, Switzerland

Peter Allen
IERC, Cranfield University, UK

Edward Elgar
Aldershot, UK – Brookfield, US

Published by
Edward Elgar Publishing Limited
Gower House
Croft Road
Aldershot
Hants GU11 3HR
UK

Edward Elgar Publishing Company
Old Post Road
Brookfield
Vermont 05036
US

British Library Cataloguing in Publication Data
Clark, Norman
Evolutionary Dynamics and Sustainable
Development: Systems Approach
I. Title
338.90011

Library of Congress Cataloguing in Publication Data
Clark, Norman.
Evolutionary dynamics and sustainable development: a systems approach / Norman Clark, Francisco Perez-Trejo, Peter Allen.
192p. 23cm.
Includes bibliographical references and index.
1. Sustainable development—Mathematical models. 2. Statics and dynamics (Social sciences)—Mathematical models. I. Perez-Trejo, Francisco. II. Allen, Peter M. (Peter Murray), 1944– .
III. Title.
HC79.E5C56 1995
333.7—dc20
95–13219
CIP

ISBN 1 85898 273 1

Printed in Great Britain at the University Press, Cambridge

Contents

Contents

Tables

Figures

Preface

This book has had rather a complicated history, stemming from the research of three individuals who come from quite different backgrounds and disciplinary expertise, but who have each become convinced of the need to explore more thoroughly a complex systems approach to policy analysis. One of us, Peter Allen, had spent a number of years as a physicist working with Prigogine and his colleagues at the Solvay Institute in Brussels. There he had been introduced to aspects of the non-linear behaviour of physical and chemical systems, and had spent the late seventies and early eighties extending these ideas to the spatial dynamics of living systems, mainly by means of models of fisheries and human settlements.

Norman Clark is a development economist who for a number of years had been working on the innovative behaviour of Third World economic systems based at the Science Policy Research Unit, the University of Sussex. Over this period he had increasingly begun to believe that conventional economic analysis was presenting obstacles to the understanding of development processes, and that the reason for this probably lay in the epistemological roots of the subject. Francisco Perez-Trejo is a systems ecologist who, for most of his career, had been working on the analysis of physical resource systems in many Third World countries. He too had been experiencing frustration with the very partial approaches conventionally used in this sort of work.

All of us had become convinced that a major difficulty with standard analytical methods and techniques is the extent to which many, if not most of them, have become very 'path-dependent' in a cognitive sense. Putting the same point rather differently many disciplines have become locked into theories, paradigms, conceptual structures and research agendas which are having increasing difficulty engaging meaningfully with the interdisciplinary nature of major world problems. For in reality, as was becoming very clear to us, the world could not be meaningfully reduced to the nostrums of this or that discipline.

In practice we had each been working in ways that may be described as 'interdisciplinary', but at the same time were becoming convinced that some form of conceptual structure was necessary to organise our efforts.

And the only promising avenue seemed to be that of general systems theory, within which notions of complexity fit quite naturally. Ideas of systemic complexity are not new, of course, stemming back as they do to the pioneering efforts of von Bertalanffy and others in the early decades of this century. However, until recently they have never influenced the mainstream of an intellectual tradition dominated by the classical mechanics of the nineteenth century.

What has changed things rather are two interrelated factors. Firstly there is the growing realisation that the behaviour of living systems (by these we mean social and natural systems by contrast with physical systems) cannot really be understood in mechanical terms. Or at least attempts to do so produce theories of the most extraordinary absurdity. Living systems are creative. They change in form and structure over time, usually with great rapidity, and it is this evolutionary property which is of most relevance to the policy maker. In contrast physical systems are effectively dead. They can function, but they do not evolve, and it is for this reason that they are capable of being understood through use of the scientific method. Living systems on the other hand are truly evolutionary. Although we can observe them in a descriptive fashion, and even discover broad behavioural regularities with which to describe them, it is difficult to come to agreed 'laws' analogous to those of the physical sciences.

The second important factor is the power of the modern computer since many analysts of living systems, aware of real-life complexity, nevertheless approximate the systems they are investigating to linear relationships on the grounds that the computational requirements of non-linear behaviour are simply too massive. Better to rely on imperfect tools of analysis than no tools at all, especially if the latter strategy leads to abuse of human systems. However, such has been the progress in computer power over the past decade that such an excuse is no longer valid, in our view.

Nevertheless there is still a marked reluctance to engage meaningfully with a complex systems approach to the analysis of issues facing living systems. Part of the reason for this is undoubtedly the existence of powerful vested interests, related both to cognitive belief systems and to institutional position. We do not underestimate the power of these. In our view, however, equally significant is the lack of analytical tools with which to engage with complexity. After all beliefs eventually change and institutional positions erode. But if we cannot actually learn to handle complexity in a practical way its existence will remain a footnote on the intellectual horizon, fascinating for those capable of playing around with pretty pictures and complicated mathematics, but of little direct significance for the human condition.

Paradoxically there are indications that some members of the scientific community would prefer it thus. For knowledge is power and the more that knowledge is confined to the chosen few the better it will be for those who are fortunate enough to be in such a position. It is interesting to speculate on the parallels between medieval religion and modern science in this regard. In his novel *The Name of the Rose*, Umberto Eco's plot takes place in a monastery, situated high up on a mountain in the north of Italy in the thirteenth century. Monasteries in those days were not unlike universities today – centres of considerable learning, enshrined in sacred texts and capable of interpretation only by a carefully chosen *'cognoscenti'*. An important sub-theme in Eco's romance relates to the monastery's library, access to which is carefully controlled by the abbot and his henchmen. Only those trusted (the 'brightest and the best'?), are allowed to enter its hallowed halls and even then under the strictest of supervision. Conversely the only real contact the masses have with the monastery is when its garbage is periodically released to tumble down the mountainside into the waiting arms of an illiterate peasantry.

It is perhaps a little unfair to make this comparison, but we could not help being struck recently by a book entitled *Complexity*,[1] which chronicles the recent foundation of a high-powered research institute at Santa Fe in the USA, set up precisely to explore this new interdisciplinary phenomenon. The whole flavour of the book is scholastic in tone, in the sense that it describes in some detail how difficult it is to move academic people out of their own disciplinary mind sets into serious engagement with radically new ideas. For many participants in this new, and exciting venture, what appears to be important is not so much the practical content of the ideas but rather how the ideas relate to established modes of thought.

Naturally this is a very stimulating project, with many able minds breaking new ground (indeed often actually *talking* to each other for the first time). And yet, we feel, there is a huge practical agenda crying out for fresh analytical insights. Problems of desertification, deforestation, pollution of waterways and soils, erosion of biodiversity, and many, many others have now begun to impinge on the world agenda with increasing urgency, and most of these are problems that result from the 'non-linear' and 'co-evolutionary' behaviour of living systems. We began to feel in a sense that the world simply cannot afford to wait while the 'experts' work out a new apparatus of thought acceptable to institutes of higher learning. The danger is that all the time they are occupied in doing this, environmental problems will become less and less amenable to remedial action. The damage will become irreversible. It may soon be too late.

And yet the complex systems approach itself suggests a possible way out. If living systems are continuously evolving, i.e. they are changing in form and structure through time, then surely it is almost axiomatic that our knowledge about them is contingent. It depends upon what part of the system you are at, how that system relates to contiguous systems and what you need the knowledge for. Another way of putting the same point is that knowledge is often largely context dependent at least to some extent, and so the people who have most to say about any given problem are very probably those immediately connected to it. What is needed, however, is some means of harnessing and mobilising such knowledge productively, some technique (or set of techniques) that will 'enfranchise the stakeholders' of that system, whoever they might be.

From this standpoint, then, there is a need for decision tools which are directly accessible to the many interests which have a stake in the system's evolution. The days are gone when the foreign expert can usefully arrive in a country with some model, or technique of universal generality and pronounce with great confidence what needs to be done. The complexity of modern living systems has made this a most undesirable practice even if it were acceptable, which generally speaking it is not. Instead we need heuristics, devices, training mechanisms (call them what you will) which permit the better formulation and conduct of policy *by those people and institutions that are directly involved.* It is our firm belief that nothing less will do. This book is our first preliminary contribution to such a project, but of course we expect to continue along these lines for some time to come. Much remains to be done.

It is important to emphasise, however, that this book is not intended as a detailed conceptual exploration of complex systems, a massive and difficult topic well beyond its scope. For example, Chapter 2 contains definitions of relevant concepts such as hierarchy, systemic openness and resilience that not everyone would accept. Even an idea as apparently straightforward as 'non-linearity' has been described by us not in terms of a non-proportional relationship between dependent and independent variables (arguably the conventional definition), but rather as indicating complicated feedback arrangements across time and space amongst a wide range of associated quantities whose precise interrelationships are not at all well understood. We make no apology for taking such a (cavalier) position since, as Gell-Mann has pointed out, ideas of complexity are still incompletely understood and subject to a great deal of debate and discussion. Indeed a good case could be made for seeing many of the associated concepts as themselves subject to evolutionary meaning as further research tightens correspondences with reality.

Rather the book should be seen as a contribution to the methodology underlying interventions in socio-economic systems – i.e. as a contribution to policy analysis and the thought processes and theoretical positions that often unconsciously underlie it, much of which we believe to be mechanistic in origin. A good example of this is the current World Bank and IMF position on structural adjustment policies for much of Sub-Saharan Africa which a range of commentators have criticised in trenchant terms (e.g. Mytelka, 1989; Stein, 1992). No one would deny that many such countries face serious problems of foreign exchange imbalance, swollen public bureaucracies, inefficient agriculture and industry, and so on. The problem is that the suggested remedies are not based on an adequate theory (or theories) of change. Instead we are usually offered highly simplistic solutions based upon the putative beneficial effects of free market regimes, solutions that not only have weak empirical foundations but in addition are often internally inconsistent and underdetermined. To repeat an analogy made elsewhere in the book, it is as if the designers of a modern battleship were offered Archimedes' Principle as their main theoretical foundation upon which to proceed.

What we are suggesting in this book is not some magical theoretical solution to these and similar problems of public policy intervention. That would be presumptuous in the extreme. What we are suggesting, however, is that a case can reasonably be made for seeing socio-economic systems as both complex and evolutionary. And from such a perspective it follows immediately that there is no such thing as simple solutions to complex problems. On the contrary, policy interventions can probably only succeed if they are founded on the direct experience and intentionality of those likely to be involved in both diagnosis and solution, the stakeholders themselves at all levels of society. Also the suggested model (as a decision tool) is only one of a range of possible approaches that could be taken in this regard, and even here a great deal more work will be needed to refine and deliver the technique if it is to have wider applicability.

It is for this reason also that readers should not become unduly alarmed by the mathematical equations in the latter half of the book. These equations have been included largely to underpin and illustrate the logic of the modelling schema adopted, but they should not deflect from the underlying arguments of the book as a whole. Those who feel uncomfortable with mathematical exposition are encouraged to avoid these passages. In fact we have tried to keep the mathematical content within the main body of the text to a minimum, relegating its fuller exposition to Appendix I.

A large number of people have provided much needed help and advice in the book's preparation and reformulation. There have been several drafts and at each stage we have benefited greatly from their criticism and encouragement. Our thanks are therefore due to Titus Adeboye, Stephen Biggs, Martin Cordey-Hayes, Ashok Desai, Christopher Freeman, Don Funnell, Mike Hobday, Anton Imeson, Calestous Juma, Sylvan Katz and William Walker. We are also especially grateful to Ana Saez for her assistance in preparing the VENSIM modelling environment described in Appendix II, and to Yuejin Tan of the Changsa Institute of Technology, China, who reformulated the original Senegal model into a version that included a separate investment function. This is described in Appendix I.

We would also like to thank Edward Arnold (Publishers) Ltd for permission to reproduce an amended version of P.M. Allen, N.G. Clark and F. Perez-Trejo (1992), 'Strategic Planning of Complex Economic Systems', *Review of Political Economy*, 4 (3), pp. 275–90 which appears in the text as Chapter 4, and Beech Tree Publishing Ltd for permission to reproduce some pages of text which are due to appear in N.G. Clark, 'The Interactive Nature of Knowledge Systems', *Science and Public Policy*, forthcoming December 1995.

Finally, grateful thanks are due to Miss Allison Bailey for her assistance with preparation of an extremely complex manuscript, and for her patience and skill in converting our draft text into a polished final product.

NOTE

1. See Waldrop (1993).

1. Modelling Sustainable Development

1.1 INTRODUCTION

This short book is about the integrated management of social and natural systems with the aid of non-linear models as decision tools and with special reference to issues of economic development in Third World countries. As such its aims are very practical although at times the reader may find the approach taken quite theoretical. It has been written as a contribution to the growing debate about environmental sustainability which achieved international prominence at the United Nations Conference on Environment and Development held at Rio de Janeiro in 1992. The book's main theme is the need to explore the issue of global sustainability in terms of the co-evolution of *both* socio-economic *and* natural systems. One of the primary difficulties in policy intervention at this level has always been the many different professional interests and cognitive perspectives brought to bear on any given problem. For example, economists see things in terms of interactions between traditional 'economic' variables such as consumption, investment, prices, employment and so forth, while many natural scientists may concentrate more on physical phenomena like soil erosion, water stress and related topographical characteristics. Similarly representatives of different ministries and other agencies will often differ considerably in their analytic view of causes, solutions and suitable policies (Gass and Biggs, 1993).

It is for this reason that our starting point is an attempt to picture the whole system and its evolutionary properties rather than those of its parts – an attempt that at first sight may appear somewhat ambitious. However, such is the contemporary need for a 'dialogue of discourse' that we felt it necessary at least to make the attempt. The decision to hinge the whole exercise on a modelling approach was taken for a similar reason. While we are very conscious that many readers are uncomfortable with mathematical models, they do nevertheless have a number of distinct advantages. In particular they can provide a point of entry, as it were, into the underlying logic of the system's evolution provided (as we try to show) that continuous attempts are made to ensure that there is some reasonable correspondence between model and reality. Moreover, compared to many economic models we should argue that our own has at least two distinct advantages. Firstly it explicitly seeks to explore the micro/macro interface. Secondly a deliberate attempt is made to keep things as simple as possible, the ultimate aim being to use the model as an aid to understanding a constantly evolving reality rather than as a mechanical representation of a reality that does not change.

The overall need for fresh thinking in this area does not require justification. The globalisation of the world economy plus growing population pressures in many of its parts, is now placing great strains on the sustainability of the global natural system (Redclift, 1987). In those areas where modern practices have been introduced, the problems relate to the impact of agro-technologies (e.g. large irrigation systems) where the consequences may become both damaging and irreversible. The destruction of parts of the Amazonian rain forest may be the example that tends to hit the headlines, but there are many other, perhaps less dramatic, cases that could be cited to make exactly the same point. Thus the effects of insecticides on traditional species of flora and fauna and the growth of soil erosion as a result of deforestation are just two of many examples that could be given of how modern practices can impinge irreversibly on the natural habitat, often threatening the biodiversity of agricultural regions (World Resources Institute, 1992).[1]

In areas relatively untouched by modern methods the environmental problems are of a different kind. For example, traditional 'slash and burn' subsistence technologies in many rural areas are no longer compatible with the shorter fallow periods enforced by rising populations and increasingly intensive patterns of livestock raising. With virtually unchanging technology the inevitable result is long-term degradation of soil fertility especially in mature ecosystems (Kiriro and Juma, 1991). Many of these dangers achieved international prominence with the publication of the report of the World Commission on Environment and Development (also known as the Brundtland Commission) in the volume entitled *Our Common Future* (1987) which drew attention to the interlinked nature of development processes (see also Juma and Cable, 1992). It states that 'until recently, the planet was a large world in which human activities and their effects were neatly compartmentalised within nations, within sectors ... and within broad areas of concern. ... These compartments have begun to dissolve'.[2]

The two most worrying features of these trends, in our view, are first their *uncertain* nature – no one is quite sure about the extent of their future impact – and second the *irreversibility* of whatever the impact will be. The effects of insecticides on traditional species of flora and fauna, the loss of traditional seed land races, and the growth of soil erosion as a result of deforestation, are just a few of many examples that could be given of how modern agricultural practices can impinge irreversibly on the natural habitat. Similarly with the impact of international tourism on water supplies. There is no doubt whatsoever that our collective capacity to manage our natural resources is at the same time both so limited and so much needed. Hence the emphasis placed in this book on the development of appropriate decision tools.

At present the main types of decision tools used for natural resource management tend to reflect tools of project appraisal, often associated with cost/benefit analysis and sometimes involving environmental impact assessment.[3] For example, Pearce et al. (1992) discuss in some detail how standard project appraisal techniques may be modified to ensure sustainability through the use of specific numerical quantities designed to capture effects on natural capital, particularly through manipulation of the social discount rate, i.e. the rate at which planners discount streams of net benefit in the future. They argue, however, that such techniques do not in general preserve natural resources and that in 'many developing countries the stocks of such resources are below any reasonable estimate of what the long-run optimal stock is'.[4] Indeed manipulation of the social discount rate can often make matters worse from a sustainability point of view.[5] Instead they propose sustainability criteria at a programmatic level in which projects that deplete natural capital are compensated by other shadow projects whose aim is to compensate for the environmental damage from the (depleting) projects in the (overall programme) portfolio.[6]

We have no quarrel with the development and use of such decision tools, which in sum represent a series of welcome attempts to build environmental considerations into project planning. Indeed at one level our own ideas should be considered as a contribution to such efforts. Where we believe we are taking matters a little further is in setting the decision problem within a wider systemic framework. The advantage of setting the decision problem in a complex systems framework is precisely that the problem cannot be viewed in isolation from the wider environment, but instead as part of an evolutionary continuum involving both the natural and the socio-economic system. In this way, too, we believe that decision tools can be made more accessible to a wider range of actors including importantly those liable to be directly affected by the implementation of any given project.

At a broader level there is a big literature on policy and policy making within the context of Third World countries, a literature that spans many academic disciplines. We do not intend to engage substantively with this literature except in the sense of arguing that much of it does not present any account of system evolution. All too often it tends to lead the reader into rather sterile debates of an ideological character where what seems to be important is as much the political position of the analyst as the likely effectiveness of this or that policy. We believe that an important reason behind such a tendency is an unwillingness to engage with the underlying evolutionary nature of natural and social systems (Clark, 1990a) on the one hand, and the inherent difficulties of applying generic scientific principles on the other. Instead of simply accepting the fundamental difference between these systems, on the one hand, and physical systems on the other – namely, the latter effectively do not evolve – there is often a tacit aim to view them as qualitatively, and therefore epistemologically, the same. The inevitable result is either to oversimplify them, and their analysis, dramatically, or to try to build models which are far too complicated to be of any practical use whatsoever to the policy maker.

At various points in the text we shall return to this theme, but at this stage it is useful to touch on a related criticism which is not quite the same, but which begins to put the problem in a more general perspective. This is the argument made by a number of analysts that intervention in socio-economic systems tends often to be of an unduly 'top-down' or 'expert' nature, with not enough attention being paid to the tacit knowledge of local stakeholders. A very good example of this broad position may be seen in Long and Long's (1992) recent edited volume on the sociology of development. This is a valuable text which makes many important points about the uses and abuses of theory and practice in the service of development. In particular the authors argue strongly against what they describe as 'structural' approaches to the study of development and social change. By this they mean methods of analysis which implicitly assume the correctness of externally generated models – i.e. models that do not take into account the (relatively autonomous) behaviour of a wide range of relevant stakeholders who are part of the system under analysis.

Instead they argue in favour of an 'actor perspective' which stresses also the additional need to investigate all those agencies, individuals and social groups that have a stake in how the system evolves. For example, they believe there is little point in planning the installation of a new irrigation system as some kind of neutral, technical project without at the same time having regard to the various ways stakeholders will try to manipulate the system in the service of their individual interests. History is full of examples where such plans have gone awry simply because of the inevitable machinations of intelligent and determined interest groups. Long and Long's view is that this has frequently been allowed to happen because decisions have been taken as if the investment can be regarded as a kind of 'black box', independent of the exigencies of social complexity. Their solution is to engage the direct and 'reflexive' participation of all relevant actors in all important policy decisions, including analysts themselves who have their own 'cognitive' axes to grind.

A similar perspective is taken by Ostrom and her colleagues. For example, in a recent book Ostrom (1990)[7] is concerned with the problems associated with the management of common-pool resources (CPRs) – i.e. resources that are not owned by specific individuals or other private economic agents, but are in some sense collectively owned by the community. Nor incidentally are they to be confused with 'public goods' like defence, which are inherently non-rivalrous and non-excludable. Rather they are resources like water or grazing lands which need to be managed in the general interests of the community as a whole.   The 'tragedy of the commons' (Hardin, 1968; Hardin and Baden, 1977) is that if some collective management does not take place then each individual will overuse the resource in question and irreversible environmental degradation will normally ensue. The reasons for this concern assumptions about the expected behaviour of rational individuals in the face of the competing behaviour of others, about risk perceptions of such economic agents and about the limited possibilities for regeneration often experienced in natural resource systems. Ostrom shows how many diverse public policy issues from fishery and firewood crises to the problems associated with 'acid rain', are of this broad generic type.

The book's main argument is that traditional ways of analysing CPR issues are on the whole too simplistic. They do not adequately capture the diversity of experience encountered despite the insights they have generated.   Another way of putting the same point is that they do not adequately engage with the complexity of the systems involved and this is mainly due to a lack of supportive empirical research. The book then goes on to chronicle a variety of case studies from which the author infers a range of provisional regularities about the management of CPRs.

There are two main types of model conventionally used to analyse CPR management. One[8] is the famous 'prisoner's dilemma' (PD) in which competing, non-cooperating and non-communicative agents with complete information about the system under analysis, act so as to produce outcomes that are third best for all of them. The paradox is that 'individually rational strategies lead to collectively irrational outcomes [which] seems to challenge a fundamental faith that rational human beings can achieve rational results'.[9] Of course the withdrawal of the key assumption (i.e. that of complete information) makes the model very problematic indeed from a scientific standpoint, but as Ostrom points out, the PD model has been used mainly in a metaphorical sense, in particular to sanction the use of a central authority to manage CPRs.

The second model is that of the efficiency of the market mechanism in the allocation of resources and the concomitant establishment of individual property rights to CPRs – the so-called privatisation option. The argument here is that many of the problems of CPR management could be solved by allocating CPRs to individual economic agents and allowing market forces to produce 'efficient' outcomes. Needless to say, this 'solution' has also proved less than perfect for a whole host of reasons connected to the sheer difficulty in practice of dividing up CPRs. For example, in the case of fisheries where the actual location of the fish is generally both unknown and unstable, it is not at all clear 'what the establishment of private rights means'.[10] In fact neither extreme option has been shown to be very successful. Indeed in some cases policies developed on the basis of too literal application of both metaphors appear to have led to worse outcomes than would have obtained had the CPRs been left to traditional modes of exploitation.

This is Ostrom's point of departure. Her starting point is the observation that throughout history and across many parts of the world there are plenty of examples of communities coming together to manage CPRs, apparently successfully. This being the case her research question is the empirical one of assessing why this should be so, a question she tries to resolve through a series of case studies. This question is then broken down further into two generic sub-questions: (i) how are problems of access to CPRs solved, the *appropriation* question, and (ii) how do appropriators ensure the sustainability of the CPR, the *provision* question. The first set consists of how to ensure equitable access to the resource on the part of all participants and how to monitor the system in a cost-effective way. The second set consists of how to maintain the necessary investment in the system such that it continues to provide an adequate flow of resources to the community. Here again there are important issues of equity and control involved since there are often temptations to 'free ride' on CPR resources.

Ostrom shows how the solution to such problems is itself a variable depending upon a range of factors such as the nature of the resource, the understanding of its systemic behaviour on the part of the community, shared norms and commitments, history, and so on. It lies in the creation of institutions specially designed in each set of circumstances to permit the members of the community, whoever they might be, to mobilise, allocate, monitor and otherwise appropriate CPRs in ways that ensure equity, sustainability and communal acceptability. Finally the book ends by suggesting a framework for the analysis of CPRs. This stresses the conditions under which stakeholders successfully agree to alter CPR rules to cope with changing situations, like growing water shortages, for example. These relate to factors such as common agreement about the pressing need to do something rather than nothing, equality of resultant impact, low levels of associated costs and the smallness and homogeneity of the community in question. Of course these conditions will obviously be affected by contextual factors like the presence of a strong political authority or how densely populated the external environment is. They will also be influenced by possibilities for external mediation and dispute resolution (Chapman, 1991). Above all, however, any framework will only serve as the beginning of a complex process which must crucially involve the direct participation of the stakeholders themselves and their unique understanding of their own specific conditions.

Although there may well be practical problems associated with this position and that of Long and Long (i.e. in the policy-making sense), we have a great deal of sympathy with them, and indeed explore briefly some of their aspects later in the text.[11] However, we believe that both critiques miss out a crucial component, namely that of an account of the real system under analysis. For if everyone has an interest in manipulating the system in his own interests, then surely there must be some common understanding of what it is that is actually being manipulated. It is precisely at this point that some kind of model is needed which can act as an aid to discourse among concerned stakeholders. We believe very much that in the absence of such a means for engaging with reality there will always be a strong tendency for policy debates to degenerate quickly into cognitive struggles between people with competing ideological views.[12]

1.2 ECONOMIC MODELS

The main reason, therefore, why it is necessary to concentrate on models is one of defining the economic system to be analysed in as unambiguous a way as possible. Such a model may then be used as the basis for appropriate decision tools. And we use the word 'appropriate' advisedly to indicate the need for correspondence with how the system in question actually works. To take a simple analogy, when we employ a plumber to install a new central heating system in our house we do so in the expectation that he has a good understanding of the intrinsic nature of domestic hot water systems and that the tools he uses are suitable for intervention in such systems. We would not, for example, be very happy if he arrived for the job carrying only a portable computer. In similar fashion all acts of development planning presume some understanding of the economic system that is being acted upon. The problem is, however, that there is not the same degree of consensus about the true nature of economic system behaviour in general, nor *a fortiori* in any specific case.

Let us begin, therefore, by exploring briefly the nature of economic models. Normally these are macroeconomic in scope – they seek to model the whole system as a set of interrelationships amongst important aggregates. Both the aggregates, as well as the patterns of their interactions, are conceptualised in terms of received theory, i.e. the equations that describe them conform to the well-established way that economists have of looking at the world. Moreover the aggregates themselves (e.g.

unemployment, investment, national output and its rate of growth, inflation, the rate of interest and so on) are usually important from a policy perspective since they facilitate predictions and legitimate specific courses of government action.

A good example of a simple dynamical model, even if it is now a little dated, is that explored by Harrod in his analysis of macroeconomic instability in a fully integrated economic system, first put forward in 1939 (Sen (ed.), 1971). Harrod showed how advanced industrial systems would normally grow in a highly unstable manner given a range of initial assumptions about the behaviour of productive and household sectors. His work led to controversy about the precise degree of this instability – about the conditions under which stabilisation would automatically come about, about the rate of fluctuation obtaining and about the proper role of government in ensuring reasonably steady growth through time.

The simplest exposition of the Harrod instability problem (and the associated conditions for a 'steady-state' equilibrium growth path) may be seen using a simple model of two linear equations one of which, the investment function, has a single period lag. The exposition also has the advantage of showing how typically economists tackle such questions (Clark and Juma, 1992). Much of the subsequent work in this field has revolved around relaxing the assumptions that underlie this sort of model, and exploring the conditions under which the outcomes might be different. The analysis can become very complex, but it is probably fair to state that most of this literature is still very much what Harrod and his colleagues initially intended it to be, namely an extension of macroeconomic instability controversies from the short into the long period. Certainly, its predisposition to describing the properties of various classifications of growth paths within an integrated industrialised economy, the classifications being dependent upon arbitrary initial assumptions and subsequent behavioural postulates, give it a distinctly artificial flavour. 'Technology', for example, is simply defined in terms of ratios of real inputs of factor services per unit of output, and 'technical change' then becomes an assumption (or set of assumptions) about how technical conditions change in specific factor-saving directions. There is, however, no real sense in which we can imagine technology as a living process, alterations to which, by government policy, will bring about changes in growth rates.

Growth models in the present day and age are much more complicated of course.[13] For example, the Cambridge Growth Project (CGP) model has over 5,000 exogenous and 500 endogenous variables, and around 16,000 parameters and coefficients (Wallis (ed.), 1987). Nevertheless they have in common a range of generic features which it is useful to summarise at this stage. The first point to make is that such models abstract from reality and hence represent merely logical constructs. For any specific model, the nature of the abstractions reflects the theoretical position of the modeller and is therefore to that extent selective. Two further properties are that underlying assumptions need to be mutually consistent and that the model should be empirically testable. The latter is important, of course, since otherwise the model would become merely an artifact of the modeller's theoretical position. A model's testability permits its predictions, and hence its assumptions, to be interpreted by a peer group. In this way the act of modelling improves dialogue and debate (George, 1988).

One problem with economic models, however, is that tests rarely allow unambiguous conclusions to be reached and since assumptions are usually a reflection of deeply held beliefs, there is a strong tendency for many conventional economic models to act as reflections of ideological positions just as much as tools of analysis. For example, there are now seven well-established models of the UK economy each of which, in addition to being differentiated *technically* from its rivals, has its own unique set of theoretical assumptions about how the economy *naturally* works. No amount of empirical research has so far managed to persuade any of these modelling groups that its own model should give way to that of one of its rivals. Nor is it likely to.

A second (related) problem, and one which in our view is even more fundamental, is the mechanical nature of most economic models. By this we mean that they are generally constructed on the assumption that the system in question does not evolve. This allows parameters to be uniquely defined as unchanging system 'descriptors' which can then be estimated statistically. The system's variables, conversely, change as the system behaves and so can be suitably isolated from a policy standpoint. We shall deal with this issue in much more detail later in the text but at this stage we shall merely stress that we do not accept the validity of this assumption. Structural changes in economic systems are a fact of life. Any attempt to hide behind a system's parameters is certain to compromise the validity of policy interventions based on a narrow, mechanistic form of economic modelling.

The third major problem we should like to highlight at this point in the text is that standard economic models by definition do not engage with 'non-economic' categories. The word 'exogenous' is often used in this respect. For example, the natural system, how it behaves and how it evolves is usually labelled 'land' and tends only to enter an economic model as an exogenous variable – that is, as something whose behaviour is not allowed to be influenced by the model's operations. Similar treatment is normally accorded to the tastes of consumers and to the technical conditions facing producers. Of course there is a good reason for such abstractions. Models are complicated things. Measures to simplify them are often necessary to facilitate the work of the modeller. Again we shall argue, however, that such facility can be bought at too high a price and that other approaches are possible.

Fourthly economic models tend to be determinate. By this we mean that provided the number of its unknown variables is no greater than the number of its equations, then the model will always have at least one unique solution. In the case of dynamical models this means future values of key policy variables, like the rate of unemployment or the level of national output, can be exactly estimated. We shall explore this feature in some detail later in the text, in particular arguing that since the reality of economic systems is their essential indeterminateness, it is misleading to try to impose this degree of rigour. Since reality is constantly changing it is much more fruitful to work with a flexible model.[14]

Finally to our knowledge there is only one economic model that deals comprehensively with the relations between the microstates and the macrostate of an economic system (Eliasson, 1991). Since we believe that such interactions play a fundamental role in system evolution, our attempt to model them is central to our approach. Indeed it is the decision making at the level of individual microeconomic agents, the households and the firms, that really drives the whole system forward. Often action designed to achieve economic advantage is subsequently found to have been mistaken. Perceptions of future events were in reality misconceived for many reasons and so new action takes place. Evolution is thus a continuous dialogue between microeconomic action and macroeconomic context, a dialogue that never ends. And unless the models we use to guide system interventions take this into account, they will always be compromised to a considerable degree.

1.3   DEVELOPMENT MODELS

Development models may be regarded as a particular species of growth model. They are concerned principally with the capacity for economic change in Third World countries – that is, countries which in some sense have not yet achieved the degree of economic power enjoyed by the industrialised countries of the north and west, but whose ambitions are broadly in this direction. The notion of development is actually quite difficult to define since not everyone can agree about matters like the nature of 'underdevelopment' or about what constitutes 'economic change'. The position taken in this book is one of defining *development as a process of structural change in economic systems*, a process which usually increases the capacity of such systems to supply goods and services to their citizens. Normally this brings along with it industrialisation as an intrinsic component, since development increases both the sheer range of commodities and the degree of 'roundaboutness' of production processes.

In an important sense, therefore, structural change implies growing *complexity*. The process of development is one of the gradual evolution from simple production systems based on subsistence agriculture, rudimentary technologies and political structures that depended on the ownership of land, to what we now recognise as the modern industrialised economy (Clark, 1985). As we progress towards the close of the twentieth century, the pace of change has become yet more rapid with the advent of new generic technologies, such as microelectronics and biotechnology, which are beginning to radically transform possibilities for economic production and distribution (Clark and Juma, 1991). Nowadays the key ingredient seems to be that of information and how it may be used for economic purposes. In this context the globalisation of the international economy testifies to the associated impact of information technology.

Modelling such an evolutionary process, however, has not proved easy, mainly because it is difficult to capture statistically the concept of 'structure', in ways that allow modelling to proceed. This is not to say, however, that there have not been many attempts to capture the idea of structure theoretically – that is, as a series of 'stories' or 'metaphors' about how development normally takes place as a process of structural change. The way this is done is to split any economic system into sectors of output origin or destination (for example, into agriculture, industry and services; or capital goods and consumer goods; or exports *vis-à-vis* domestic production and so on), and then to use these as a point of departure for theoretical discussion (Chaudhuri, 1989).

A good example to illustrate this procedure is the well-known attempt by Arthur Lewis (1963) to explain economic development in terms of the gradual absorption into the modern industrialised sector of an abundant, low productivity labour reserve employed mainly in subsistence agriculture. Lewis believed that the problem of development really boiled down to one of how to provide the right types of social mechanism which would permit this to happen efficiently, in particular stressing the importance of national savings and the creation of incentives and institutions to transfer these savings to capitalist entrepreneurs who would then employ underutilised labour more productively (Hunt, 1989).

A better-known example of the same 'genre', and one incidentally that influenced Lewis's own views, is Marx's famous account of capitalist economic development,[15] which he saw as proceeding inexorably towards a series of ever worsening crises. According to Marx the annual output of any economic system is distributed between the following three categories.

- An amount necessary to replace depreciated capital stock. Marx

called this 'constant capital' (*c*).
- An amount necessary to pay the wage bill of labour called 'variable capital' (*v*).
- An amount left over for the 'surplus value' (*s*) accruing to capitalists.

Hence in general national income (*y*), which is equivalent to national output, is given by:

$$y = c + v + s \qquad (1.1)$$

Marx went on to use this broad generic relationship to underpin a whole series of analytic predictions of macroeconomic behaviour such as, for example, that of a tendency towards a falling rate of profit in all branches of economic production. Thus using (1.1) he defined:

s/v = s =   the rate of surplus value
$c/(c + v)$ = q =   the organic composition of capital
$s/(c + v)$ = p =   the rate of profit

p can then be defined in terms of *s* and *q* as follows:

$$p = s/(c + v) = sv/v(c + v) = [s(c + v) - sc]/v(c + v)$$
$$= s/v - s/v[c/(c + v)] = s(1 - q) \qquad (1.2)$$

The rate of profit is thus directly proportional to the rate of surplus value and inversely proportional to the organic composition of capital. Marx believed that the rate of surplus value would tend to remain stable but that capital accumulation (driven by business competition) would bring about a rising *q* which in turn would lead to a falling rate of profit.

There are many examples of this style of analysis of the structural change of economic systems. What they all have in common is a set of simplifying assumptions about the natural behaviour of economic agents, *in the aggregate*, as generators of change under specific technical conditions. Usually they also embody strong ideological beliefs, as we have said. What they tend not to do as a whole is to lend themselves easily to empirical verification. Many of Marx's predictions, for example, became articles of faith for generations of scholars who could always find reasons why lack of empirical correspondence obtained. This lack of intellectual 'symbiosis' between theory and evidence is, in our view, a major drawback which we have attempted to tackle through our own approach of using models as decision tools rather than as precise representations of reality.

Finally it is useful just to mention at this stage that a number of economic statisticians have attempted to capture historic structural change in a much more direct fashion. Probably the most famous of these is Simon Kuznets (1959) whose accounts of long-term international economic growth patterns have now become standard works of reference. For example, using cross-section and time-series studies, Kuznets was able to establish the shift from agriculture into industry and services that characterises most economic growth. He also concluded that as per capita income rises, inequality in income distribution rises at first but then falls off. What is perhaps interesting about this type of work is how relatively divorced it is from 'grand theory'. Indeed Kuznets became famous subsequently for throwing cold empirical light on some of the grander claims of some of his theoretical peers.

1.4 SPATIAL DEVELOPMENT AND THE ENVIRONMENT

Perhaps the most important drawback, however, in conventional models of economic development is that very little mention is made of the spatial dimension. Analysis is conducted almost exclusively in terms of economic space and time.[16] And yet it is perhaps the uneven impact of economic development on a regional basis which is proving to be most crucial from a policy standpoint, as we have outlined briefly above. There are two aspects to be considered here. One is the practice of model builders to exclude geographical factors from temporal growth models. The other is that of relegating the environment to an exogenous status – that is, not including it as an integral part of the modelling schema. Both are related problems but require separate discussion, at least to begin with.

On the first aspect it is perhaps a little unfair to put things in precisely this way since demographers and geographers have done a great deal of interesting research to explain patterns of spatial change in economic activity (Leloup, 1993). For example, central-place models have been influential in explaining and predicting the distribution of markets across regions on a hierarchical basis, while gravity models have been widely used to explore the influence of distance on flows of commodities and people. Also within economic analysis of underdeveloped regions there is a tradition which examines spatial aspects – compare, for example, the writings of Gunnar Myrdal (1957) and the models linking migration and economic development associated with the names of Lewis, Fei, Ranis, Pack, Todaro and others (Hunt, 1989).

We would argue, however, that much of this work (with the possible exception of Myrdal's) does not really engage with economic complexity despite the many insights it has provided. Our position may be summarised in the following way. Much of the behaviour of economic agents is conceived in aggregate terms tending towards equilibrium states of the macro system. In the case of Ranis and Fei (1961), for example, one of their principal conclusions relates to the precise conditions under which a balanced growth path between 'modern' and 'traditional' sectors will be realised. The labour force is homogeneous and its behaviour is 'average'; it does not exhibit any microscopic diversity. We shall try to deal specifically with this point later in the text.

The question of environmental exogeneity is much more difficult to handle because it concerns the tricky problem of defining the boundaries of the economic system under discussion. The traditional position taken by many economists is that this should be defined purely in terms of the production, distribution and consumption of measurable goods and services, that is, commodities to which property rights can be assigned and which can thus be exchanged in markets using money as a medium of exchange (there are difficult questions about how to deal with 'public goods' but this does not alter the general position taken). Defined in this way, *other* costs and benefits arising from any given transaction are treated as so-called 'external effects' – that is, as impinging *outside* the system's boundaries. They are not, therefore, capable of analysis by the tools of the economics profession though this does not mean that they do not have practical significance.

This position has become less and less tenable in recent years, however, mainly because these external (sometimes called 'secondary') effects are beginning to become much more widely felt as a result of the industrialisation of the international economy. Some economists (like David Pearce and his colleagues (1989) at the University of London) have responded by arguing forcefully that it is nevertheless possible to consider environmental issues within the broad economics paradigm, that is, by using specific quantitative techniques like cost/benefit analysis. In particular, as we outlined near the beginning of this chapter, they argue that where there is clear evidence of externalities, these may be 'internalised' using traditional tools of economic policy which have the effect of relating them more directly to relevant economic actors. For example, where it can be shown that a specific factory is polluting the environment with noxious substances, 'end-of-pipe' taxes can be levied to pay the associated social costs. More generally a policy regime like this will provide an appropriate set of incentives for business behaviour.

While there are, we believe, considerable advantages in this approach compared to the traditional one – in the sense that it is better to have some accounting for social costs than none at all – there is nevertheless some way still to go. One problem is certainly that of establishing credible quantitative indicators as Norgaard (1985) and others have stressed at length. More serious are a range of difficulties that can only be described as methodological. What we mean by this is that the methods used by most economists do not rest upon any account of how the system under analysis actually evolves. Nor is there any parallel account of its co-evolution with that of the natural system. And yet an integrated treatment of problems of environmental change surely requires such an account. Our own approach to such matters is to try to define explicitly what is meant by the term 'system', independent of the context in which it is being used, and to establish its generic properties as an exercise prior to model construction. In this way not only is it possible to model the co-evolution of the economy and its environment, it is also possible to draw more general conclusions about the practical evolution of economic systems and thus improve policy prescription.[17]

1.5   THE SCIENTIFIC METHOD

A final point to stress in this introductory chapter, and one that is in a sense closely related to the points made in the previous paragraph, is that of the implications of our approach in a more general sense. We take the view that economic systems, like all natural systems, are in a constant state of evolution. Their structure is constantly changing and so is incapable of exact definition. Hence, as we mentioned above, unlike physical systems, economic systems do not lend themselves easily to description in terms of parameters and variables. The best we can say is that a typical economic system's parameters are likely to change more slowly than its variables. And to that extent parametric estimates must therefore always be contingent.

Hence while the canons of science apply quite well to relatively stable physical systems, the same is not true of economic systems. Modelling the latter is like trying to hit a 'moving target'. And the models we use must inevitably be proximate and revisable analytical tools. It follows that the capacity of a model to make an exact 'prediction' is not *by itself* a good test of its usefulness. What is much more important is its accessibility to the various actors whose understanding of its inner working is so crucial to policy intervention. Indeed such is the rate of change of modern economic structures that economic forecasts are almost always expected to be wrong. It would be very surprising indeed if they turned out to be correct. Nor has this actually happened in the case, for example, of the seven UK economic models mentioned above.

More important perhaps is the need for explicit recognition that how we search for and use knowledge in policy intervention must also be changed. For if socio-economic systems experience rapid structural change then it is no longer acceptable for 'expertise' to be introduced *only* from on high, so to speak, to those charged with system intervention. What is now needed also are the means to monitor and control complex evolutionary changes through a continuous dialogue between research and practice. For far too long social science has been 'long on analysis but short on intervention', policy being something conveniently left to the decision maker. On the contrary, it is a fundamental argument of this book that the recognition of policy making as a social process is not only urgently needed in a practical sense, it is actually a necessary corollary to the correct use of the scientific method when applied to the analysis of economic systems. We close our argument in Chapter 6 with a restatement of this important point.

1.6   LAYOUT

Returning then to the discussion at the beginning of the chapter, our main objective in this book is to suggest a class of decision tools which can be used to manage the sustainable development of economic systems. Notice, however, that as the chapter has progressed we have begun increasingly to define development as an *integrated process of structural change* rather than as one of economic growth *per se*. It is not so much the rate of growth of some economic quantity, like Gross Domestic Product (GDP), that is important but rather the emergence of different types of industrial and social institution, the corresponding advent of new technologies, changes in patterns of land use, new structures of governance and other alterations in the pattern of the social fabric. 'Development', in our view, is much too rich a concept to be summarised under specific empirical measures. It is largely for this reason that our conceptual approach will be based on a variant of general systems theory rather than that of the economic analysis which normally informs this type of discussion, although at various points in the text we relate our arguments to more standard theories of economic development.

   A second point to be made at this stage is that we do not engage to any significant extent with much of the modern literature on the influence of new technology on Third World economic development, a literature that has grown very fast indeed in recent years.[18] We should emphasise that this omission does not belie its importance. On the contrary, we agree with the proposition that technological change, broadly defined, is probably *the* most important factor contributing to better economic performance. However, there are two reasons at least why detailed discussion has been left out of our treatment. One is that much of the recent literature relates directly to *industrial* development, whereas our focus concentrates primarily on issues of natural resource management. Secondly, the dynamical models we have been developing have not yet reached the sophistication required for the direct incorporation of technical change into them. Having said this, however, readers should note the brief discussion of recent neo-Schumpeterian contributions in Chapter 3 and our references to the 1970s literature on World Dynamic models in Chapter 6.

The general layout of the book is as follows. Chapter 2 represents our attempt to define systems independently of their analytical context and through this a number of important generic properties concerning structure, function and evolution. Particular attention is paid to relative openness, stability, adaptability, complexity, hierarchy and evolutionary drive. Chapter 3 goes on to explore economic systems as complex systems. The emphasis here is one of placing economic analysis in a systemic framework before going on to contrast its mechanistic and evolutionary properties. Although there has been some progress in recent years in its capacity to handle questions of growth and change, our conclusion is that the economics profession as a whole is still too strongly wedded to its neo-classical roots to deal adequately with complex issues of structural change of the type we have outlined above. Accordingly we set out in some detail an alternative approach which is consistent with the material covered in Chapter 2.

Chapter 4 then presents a broad type of modelling procedure involving the spatial and temporal evolution of an economic system which is then integrated with that of the natural system. The approach is an explicit attempt to integrate analysis at micro and macro levels while at the same time providing a decision tool of use to the policy analyst. After laying out the model in mathematical terms we go on to its general properties and how it can be calibrated. Chapter 5 applies the model to a particular case – that of the Crete economy in recent years. A number of planning scenarios are investigated with special emphasis on the likely long-term effects of tourism expansion, particularly with reference to prospects for employment and for environmental degradation. Finally Chapter 6 goes on to examine what we feel we have learned from the case study in a more general sense, returning to the methodological issues raised in the early parts of the book.

NOTES

1   See also Sanchez and Juma (1994).
2   WCED (1987), p. 4.
3   We shall not be considering the use of traditional decision tools in any detail. Those interested should consult Pearce et al. (1992) for extensions of social cost/benefit analysis (SCBA), Biswas and Agarwal (eds) (1992) for the application of environmental impact assessment (EIA) techniques to developing countries, and Lee (ed.) (1992) for approaches that favour strategic environmental impact assessment. A paper that tries to reconcile the respective merits of SCBA and EIA is that of van Pelt

(1993) who argues that multi-criteria analysis (MCA) is often to be preferred where data are weak, economic activities are directly dependent on natural resources and distribution concerns are important.

4   See Pearce et al. (1992), p. 37.
5   This is so mainly because a blanket reduction in the discount rate will tend in practice to encourage excessive investment of all types, thereby increasing pressures on the environment. See ibid., p. 47.
6   Ibid., p. 60. The authors note that they are indebted to Klaassen and Botterweg (1976) who, it seems, were the first to propose this criterion.
7   See also Ostrom, Schroeder and Wynne (1993).
8   Ostrom actually mentions two others of this type but they do not seem to us to be so fundamental. See Ostrom (1990), Chapter 1.
9   See Ostrom ibid., p. 5.
10 Ibid., p. 13
11 See Chapter 6
12 See, for example, Thompson (1993) who shows in graphic detail that such differences can in some circumstances cost a great deal of money.
13 For a detailed discussion of some new views about the modelling of complex systems, see Ormerod and Campbell (1993).
14 See Rosen (1987) for an interesting mathematical treatment of this issue. Using a simple predator/prey model, Rosen shows how conventional mathematics are really a special case of a broader informational mathematics which do not lead to exact solutions but which do provide a more realistic account of evolutionary change.
15 One of the best short accounts of this (which is used in what follows) is contained in Sweezy (1942).
16 But see Malecki (1991) for a comprehensive review of the literature relating to technology and spatial development.
17 It is interesting to speculate on why it is that the economics profession has had so much difficulty engaging with ideas of evolutionary complexity. Our own view is that it is based upon poor understanding of the scientific method, combined with certain specific kinds of ideological values. See for example Clark (1990a) for a further discussion of this and related points.
18 A useful summary introduction to this literature may be found in Bell and Pavitt (1993).

2. The Nature of Systems

2.1 INTRODUCTION

This chapter explores what we mean by the concept of a 'system' and how it may be described and characterised. As we mentioned in the Preface there is in fact a substantial literature on systems analysis dating back fifty years and more. For example, Lotka and von Bertalanffy began to develop an open systems perspective on all science in the 1920s and 1930s, while more recently Emery, Beer, Ashby and many others have done a great deal of valuable work in applying systemic ideas to a wide range of disciplines.[1] We do not intend to engage directly with what is obviously a long academic tradition. Nor do we believe that there is *one* definition of a system which is necessarily *the* correct one. We do feel, however, that there are important analytical reasons for setting out as clearly as possible our own views regarding the intrinsic nature of a 'system'. All too often there is a tendency for policy analysis to retreat back to the single discipline with the inevitable result that such analysis often fails to capture the holistic nature of problems and solutions. Sometimes also the concept of 'system' is used, but rarely is it unambiguously defined and often the reader is left wondering what precisely is the nature of such a system, what does it consist of, how may it be identified, how may it be classified, how does it behave, and so forth?

The main objective of this chapter is thus one of defining the concept of a system independent of the context in which it is to be applied and in such a way as to lay an analytical basis for the book as a whole. Hence typical questions to be tackled are: how and in what senses an open system may be distinguished from a closed one, how a system typically evolves in the direction of increasing complexity (what indeed do we mean by complexity?) and what implications a 'systems' view of evolutionary change may have for the scientific method? An important secondary reason for this exploration, however, is that it lays the basis for a corresponding discussion about economic systems which will take place in the following chapter, although we shall make brief references to them in this chapter.

It is important to emphasise, however, that much contemporary discussion of systems and their properties is by no means agreed on issues of exact definition. For example, the idea of *complexity* which we come to later in this chapter is actually a very difficult one to define unambiguously, as Gell-Mann (1994) has recently pointed out. Superficially it might appear that as the number of component parts of a system and their degree of interrelatedness increases (what we might call an increase in their 'complicatedness'), their complexity would also increase. But this is not necessarily the case, Gell-Mann argues.[2]   Not only is the formal mathematical relationship between these two notions non-linear, but intuitively also one can see that as certain types of system increase in their 'complicatedness' they can actually get *less complex* beyond a certain point.

A good example of this might be a social organisation such as a firm which grows beyond a certain optimum size and as a result ceases to be able to function efficiently. Organisational arteries begin to harden as established routines get embedded into the social structure, it becomes increasingly difficult to respond quickly to extra-systemic environmental influences like those associated with sudden market shifts, while internal power struggles get bogged down in a morass of conflicting vested interests on the part of component groups.

Gell-Mann's view is that under these circumstances the firm *as a productive unit* actually becomes less complex, which leads him to a definition of complexity that is somehow related to the operational efficiency of the whole system being analysed. In his view all human systems must achieve a balance between cooperative and competitive behaviour if they are to be successful, and their degree of complexity is a function of how near to optimising that balance they have come. It is not our purpose in this book, however, to get directly involved in very detailed definitional issues of this type. What we have done is to put forward our own view of the nature of a system and of its constituent properties with the primary purpose of defining the categories relevant to our overall purpose. To the extent that our readership disagrees with these definitions they must then re-interpret the body of the text accordingly. As we outlined in the Preface, however, it seems likely that general systems theory has not reached the stage where definitional consensus on many of its aspects has actually been reached. And under these circumstances, therefore, it is equally important not to get unduly sidetracked on controversies that are likely very quickly to become unproductive.

2.2 OPEN AND CLOSED SYSTEMS

At a broad descriptive level a system may be defined as something which is made up of interconnected elements, and has a boundary which separates the inside from the environment. Often a distinction is drawn between a *closed* system and an *open* system, based upon the extent to which the analyst wishes to consider the degree of interaction with the system's environment. When the system is open, both matter and energy can enter and leave the system. When the system is closed, in general energy, but not matter, can cross its boundary. Sometimes a distinction is also made between an *isolated* and a *closed* system such that in the former case neither matter nor energy can cross its boundary.

In the human or life sciences, however, in addition to these broad distinctions (which often actually help to define a system in the physical sciences as a closed one), we have three additional requirements. Firstly, the interacting elements which make up living systems are connected in an *organised* manner. Secondly, the participating components are *affected by their participation, and are modified* when they leave the system. Thirdly, the system as a whole *behaves*. It does something while turning its inputs into outputs, or depending on the point of view, it may do something in order to turn its inputs into outputs.

The difference between these two groups of definitions shows the gulf that has built up between non-living (physical) and living (natural and social) systems. In addition, we may note that no living organisms can ever exist for very long in isolation. They all require a flow of energy and matter to maintain their existence. And this is an important clue to understanding the emergence of functional organisation. Thus the difference between purely physical systems on the one hand, and natural or social systems on the other, is precisely that of internal organisation, system level behaviour and an active maintenance of internal components. In fact we now know that all open systems (whether natural or social) are capable of self-organisation. Indeed such systems are capable of seeking out sources of energy and matter that they need in order to maintain their organisation. Conversely purely physical systems, like a stone for example, do not demonstrate these qualities.

2.3   LIVING SYSTEMS

Let us look more closely, then, at living systems. The first point to note is that the fundamental processes which lead to structural change in such systems are both complex and highly variable. In particular the interdependence of biospheric and atmospheric processes and their coupling to human activities are such that direct correspondence between cause and effect cannot be assumed. The basic reason for this is that the processes which collectively constitute what we perceive and describe as 'the environment', are in essence, non-linear, i.e. they are in no sense directly linked in a linear, causal chain.

It follows that the dynamics of such systems cannot be completely understood either from descriptive studies or as equilibrium systems. Instead they should be seen as a series of unpredictable responses to events where a critical role is played by feedback mechanisms which act to amplify, or reinforce human, biological, physical or socio-economic processes. Thus for example, within the context of the interaction of economic systems and the environment, we can see how the amplification of, for example, increasing subsidies – not linked to any real increase in food demands, and generating overproduction – may produce intensified pressures on the land through the cultivation of marginal land and overgrazing. In turn, these processes can lead to an acceleration of soil erosion and to general ecological deterioration. Understanding the role of such cumulative causation, then, is of critical importance to the provision of sound policy and management directives.

Another important characteristic in the study of living systems is that their dynamics are strongly influenced by the spatial patterns of their components. Interactions between different spatial and temporal scales may be thought of as comprising a hierarchy of organisational levels, such that processes operating at one level are only partially autonomously defined, because processes operating at other spatial or temporal scales can affect their dynamics (Perez-Trejo, 1989). For example, in studying the problems of erosion or salinisation in Southern Europe it was found essential not only to focus on higher-level processes, such as those induced by land-use changes and agricultural policy, but to include also a close examination of underlying activity at the level of the natural system itself, for example, changing soil structure and soil/water interaction (Perez-Trejo et al., 1993a).

2.4   RESILIENCE AND STABILITY

Another advantage that a systems perspective brings to bear on our understanding of the processes of structural change, is that it provides a framework for taking into account the role of stability/instability in system evolution. The notion of stability is itself the subject of multiple definitions but most commonly it finds expression as a condition close to, or at, an equilibrium point (Allen, 1975). However, recent ecological investigations have led to the concept of non-equilibrium ecosystems in which resilience is defined as the degree to which a system can be changed and still recover (Holling, 1973, 1985). Thus, resilience is not only concerned with the ability of the system to maintain its structure in the face of disturbance, but is also a property that allows the system to absorb and utilise change.

Putting it differently, we are not referring to the system's ability to return to some hypothetical equilibrium state in the face of some disturbance. Rather we are referring to its ability to explore possible evolutionary pathways which it *could* follow, defined in terms of different regimes of operation. Resilience, in a complex systems perspective extends, therefore, beyond the measure of what has been defined as 'return time' to a previous assumed equilibrium state.

A similar approach to the same phenomenon is Conway's distinction between 'sustainability' and 'stability' which he uses to describe agroecosystems. For Conway (1984, 1993) the key to the distinction is that of the productivity of the system in question. 'Stability measures the behaviour of an agroecosystem in response to the normal fluctuations in the surrounding environment. Productivity goes up and down but is not seriously threatened. However, agroecosystems are also subject to major disturbing forces which can cause productivity to fall well below its previous level. If productivity does fall it may recover either to its original level or to a new lower level or, in extreme situations, may cease altogether. Sustainability is the ability of an agroecosystem to withstand such disturbing forces.'[3]

There are many examples that could be used to illustrate this property of resilience (or sustainability) in natural systems. For example Mediterranean shrublands and grasslands have been shown to exist within a globally stable dynamic regime and far from equilibrium for long periods. Similarly with Caribbean forests and mangrove swamps. In more conventional terminology, these systems are characterised by low stability. Additionally, it has been shown that instabilities in population dynamics can lead to greater species diversity along with spatial patchiness – circumstances which tend towards increased resilience.

A useful illustration of the notion of resilience and the existence of multiple stable states (or what is sometimes referred to as metastability) can be seen from the accompanying illustration (Figure 2.1), which describes the movement of a marble on a hilly surface representing the response surface of the possible states of a system. The marble moving through the response surface represents one of the possible trajectories which the system may follow in its dynamics through time. What we see is that if the marble is placed on the summits at L, M, or N, then it is unstable. The most stable equilibrium position for the marble is point A, since it can descend no further. However, it can also remain at points B, C, or D, even if the system is perturbed by environmental fluctuations. By definition, points, B, C and D are metastable equilibrium positions. Moreover, the depth in the troughs represent increasing metastability at that particular point.

However, it should be pointed out that this traditional view of systems response in terms of a series of fixed 'hills' and 'valleys' representing different behaviours, is actually incomplete. In reality, the passage of a complex system from one regime of behaviour to another involves both the 'trigger' that actually pushes the system over the lip of a different basin of attraction, as well as the rest of the 'system interactions' which generate the shape of the potential surface illustrated in Figure 2.1. The chains of human decision-making, involving economic and socio-cultural phenomena, form part of this, as do physical and biological mechanisms. For example, Figure 2.2 shows the response of the surface of the system in terms of the effect of landscape development on the dynamics of its biomass, so that as the ball rolls over the surface, it actually modifies or re-creates some part of the surface itself.

Figure 2.1   Multiple states of system dynamics

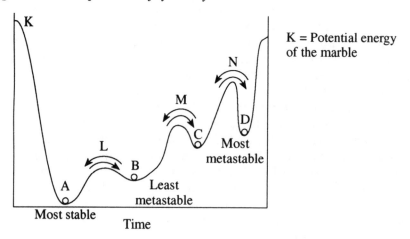

Figure 2.2   Effect of landscape development on biomass dynamics

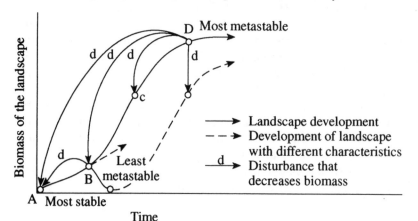

A related issue concerns the notions of adaptability and resilience in relation to complexity. Broadly speaking, the higher the degree of inherent variability which system components have accumulated as adaptive strategies, the higher the probability of system stability. This is because the degree of resilience is linked to the ability of the system's components to explore and develop mutually beneficial strategies and behaviours which will permit them to change and adapt in response to disturbance. A useful example of these concepts can be seen from recent agricultural practices in Mediterranean Europe. Here we might cite the introduction of monoculture practices (such as the introduction of sunflowers as a cash crop), as an example of a system which has been highly simplified from its original complexity, and where the natural coherence of the system has been substituted by artificial fertilizer inputs and introduced species of very little adaptability. As a result, such systems are often intrinsically unstable and characterised by low resilience. In this way monoculture systems are in direct contrast to traditional extensive systems of agriculture in which the practice of intercropping generates the kind of spatial patchiness and high adaptability associated with natural ecosystems. This problem of diminishing biodiversity is now becoming a major international issue.

2.5   CLASSIFICATION OF SYSTEMS

When faced with the problem of trying to understand the behaviour of a system such as a forest or a busy city, the first activity is probably to note the different characteristics of the objects that compose it, and to describe and measure them. But, having done that, it is then necessary to categorise them in a meaningful way. Clearly, instead of noting down every single instance of every single thing, it is usual to classify them into groups of individuals which are sufficiently similar.[4] But the question 'what is sufficiently similar?' is actually quite difficult to answer. Indeed, it poses implicitly the complementary question 'what is sufficiently different to merit its own category?'. On the one hand, an elephant is different from a mouse, in that if we examine their respective measurements even the statistical extremes are not at all overlapping. Even the largest most elephantine mouse is unlike the most mouse-like elephant. On the other hand, both a mouse and an elephant share the characteristics of mammals, which a frog does not. So, finally, whether a mouse is more like a frog than an elephant depends on the weighting we choose to give particular characteristics. It is therefore subjective, and there seems no totally objective way for a taxonomy based on 'likenesses' to be established. In addition to this, the situation is likely to be even more complicated in reality, where local populations may differ considerably in their characteristics, and indeed, individuals may cover quite a variation of type and form.

In fact, though, the merit of distinguishing one particular group from another depends on the question that is being asked. For example, the effort involved in distinguishing the many different types of phytoplanckton in a particular patch of the ocean may not change the amount of primary production occurring there, and so, if this is what affects fish catches, may be of little interest. Sometimes, however, it turns out that the presence of some particular type may be of critical importance. Usually, this can only be learned about from experience, when our usually satisfactory description fails to explain what is happening. The real question that this raises is the level of detail that is required in order to classify phenomena satisfactorily, and in addition, how it would ever be possible to anticipate the appearance of new types of entities?

In short, the problems of classification and taxonomy are extremely complex, so much so that discussion and argument about them continue to this day. There are two basic principles on which a taxonomy can be founded and each has its rival band of supporters. The first is the method we have briefly touched on above. It concentrates on the presence or absence of certain characteristics, a classification by appearances. This is called *phenetic* classification and is favoured by numerical taxonomists – people who like to count. The alternative is an evolutionary scheme or *phylogenetic* taxonomy which seeks to categorise in terms of the evolutionary closeness of the specimens considered.

This second method, in biology, is called *cladism* and seems to be more useful from the point of view of understanding living systems. This is because it focuses on the question of how living matter changed from being contained in just a few simple forms, to the immense diversity and complexity of the millions of species that we know have existed. How did this self-structuring of living matter occur? How were all these new forms created? And what are the rules which govern this extraordinary inventiveness of living matter? Looked at in this way taxonomy simply poses the problem of evolution. Somehow evolution generated these incredible changes in the structure of living matter. Somehow it invented new categories and traits, sought out new resources, fought against new constraints, and invaded new territories and dimensions. Taxonomy, and in particular evolutionary taxonomy, is an attempt to retrace backwards this amazing voyage of discovery.

One of our aims in this book is to explore the sources of this creativity with particular reference to economic systems, and to describe the first faltering attempts to include such creativity in mathematical models. As we shall see, however, in taking this step we have had to modify our previous ideas concerning both the scientific method and what we consider as the scientific explanation of an experience. Instead of science being about revealing the eternal laws which govern a system, allowing a process of prediction and verification, it turns out that science is really concerned with understanding the past of the existing system, with its characteristic spatial and temporal scales, while admitting the uncertainty that must result from its inherent ability to be creative (Allen, 1989).

As we defined it at the beginning of this chapter, a system is made up of component parts (or elements) which are connected by interactions. In a machine, this is simple. There are fixed and moving parts, with variables representing positions, velocities and momenta as well as their angular equivalents, and internal parameters concerning the materials and form of these parts. There are also environmental parameters concerning, for example, the air resistance and temperature of the surroundings. But, what of a forest, or a city? What are its components? What is the environment? Here, the problem is not as simple. Obviously, a forest is made up mostly of trees, and so we may call the trees the components. But then there are different types of tree and different size trees of the same type.

Should we use each individual tree as a separate component, and create literally a model of the forest? Or, is there some way of combining trees which are sufficiently similar into a particular class, and of describing the changes that take place in the forest in terms of the changing numbers of each class? Again whether or not this is a satisfactory solution depends on the question that you are trying to answer. If you wish to know exactly what will happen to each tree individually, then clearly the reduced description above will not do. But if you only wish to make calculations about the quantities of nuts and berries or of wood that are available, then the simpler description may well suffice.

This is the principle behind *population dynamics* (Allen, 1988). It is really quite fundamental to a lot of what we shall be thinking about. Ultimately, everything that is of normal, everyday size, is about population dynamics, because everything is made up of cells, biomolecules, atoms and elementary particles. Even if we try to describe every single tree in our forest, we shall only be performing a population dynamics approximation on the molecules and cells that make them up. Similarly for a city, the components that we choose to differentiate will depend on the questions that we wish to address. Instead of attempting to model all the different individuals, we can choose to describe the different types of people that live and work there, and how many reside or work in a particular zone. Our variables will be the value of each particular population present in each zone at a given time, and these will change over the long term as a result of births, deaths and migrations, and in the short term as a result of trips to other zones to work, shop or visit.

This introduces another key point – not only is the choice of variables dependent on the questions that are being asked, but so are the spatial and temporal scales that are used in their description. We shall see that the essential difference between variables and parameters is that the latter change on a slower time scale than the former. Some parameters reflect the nature and performance of the populations in the description, such as fertility, natural mortality, and physical capacities to travel, work and shop. However, others reflect the environment, since they concern factors which are either geographically outside the area covered by the model, or which are not considered explicitly in the variables. In the city example, the environment might include external competitors and export customers, potential investors who may locate enterprises in the city, pollution which may affect health, and various diseases which may affect birth and death rates. In addition, there are the habitual behaviours, and decision processes of the citizens, which reflect their culture and practice. There are their aspirations for example, and the concepts of the life style they seek. These may be treated as constant parameters for the study of daily behaviour, but may also be the driving forces of fundamental change in the longer term. In the end, the point which constantly returns is that understanding a system will always be an incomplete process. Once creativity exists, then we are in a universe of permanent learning, not one of permanent truth.

2.6   SYSTEM EVOLUTION

Let us now return to the question of change since it is how systems evolve that we really need to understand. The only 'law' in physics which clearly addresses the question of change and the direction of time is the second law of thermodynamics. But this is not really a 'law' like the others, since in fact it merely accepts the existence of time's arrow, of irreversibility. It neither proves that this must result from more fundamental laws, nor shows exactly how this can be reconciled with them. Evolution and change are concepts that science has traditionally been unable to deal with satisfactorily. And this is related to the choice of 'mathematics' as its preferred language of expression. Equations, however, merely express the fact that the left- and right-hand sides must be equivalent, and therefore that they are merely two different ways of saying the same thing. The 'trick' involved in mathematical descriptions of systems and their change through time, is to suppose that the left- and right-hand sides of an equation correspond to later and earlier times, respectively. In this way, the assumption of some law of 'conservation', means that earlier and later values must be identical, and therefore that if the amount of something in one part of a system increases, then there must be a compensatory decline in the amount of something else.

But such a perspective denies the existence of creativity and innovation, seeing as it does everything in terms of 'elementary particles' swirling around in space according to fundamental mechanical laws. The application of this 'traditional' kind of science to the real world, simply requires a suitable definition of the appropriate 'elementary particles' conserved over time in order to write down equations which allow prediction. Change, in this view, is the superficial transfer of these components from one part of the system to another.

But change and transformation, the emergence and evolution of complex societies, do not merely concern the changing numbers produced by some mechanical representation. Rather, they are about the spontaneous appearance of new structures and states of organisation (Allen, 1982), implying that we must recognise at least two levels of description for our system: that of its 'elementary' components subject to an 'accounting' principle, and that of the structure or organisation within which they exist. In other words our 'science' should aim at understanding the relation between these two levels if it is not to be trivial. It is the mutual co-evolution of these two levels of description that is at the heart of the matter, and our focus of concern is the emergence of such new entities, with new powers and needs, which open new dimensions of experience.

According to the view to be presented here, therefore, change is not just an occasional and rare phenomenon, but instead change, and more importantly the *capacity* to change, plays a much greater role than previously believed in 'explaining' the diversity we observe around us. The stability of any existing macroscopic form (or description) is permanently tested by the experiences of each local context. The power of self-transformation that living systems possess is a natural result of the evolutionary process itself, since evolution leads to systems which possess both the ability to evolve and the capacity to adapt and change in response to the uncertainties of the real world. This ability resides ultimately in the internal diversity and variability of populations.

Indeed, we now understand that our present circumstances are not an inevitability, but were created by their particular history, a history marked by creativity and the emergence of new forms, functionalities and organisations. More generally we can say that the natural environment of man has been constantly changing, either on its own or as a result of human activities, and of course the human environment of man (socio-cultural behaviour) has also been changing over time. It follows that the long-term survival (or extinction) of any particular group of humans is perhaps more related to its ability to cope with uncertainty and change, and to generate appropriate responses, than to the optimality of its precise behaviour at a given time.

2.7   THE EVOLUTIONARY DRIVE

One interesting method of exploring these ideas is to introduce the concept of the evolutionary drive which is common to all living populations and which has been explored in a number of recent papers by one of the authors of this book (Allen and McGlade, 1987a). The idea here is to define a 'possibility space', a space representing the characteristics and behaviours that could potentially arise for the different types of individuals present. In practice, of course, this is a multidimensional space of which we would only be able to anticipate a few of the principal dimensions. However, it is nevertheless extremely instructive to think about the evolutionary process in these terms. The central problem of change is that of understanding how, over time, the kinds of behaviour present in a system can actually increase and complexify. In terms of 'possibility space', the question is 'if initially there is a single type of individual present, occupying a single cell of this space, then how can new populations appear?'.

The answer clearly, is that this 'possibility space' will be explored by individuals whose behaviour is plastic in some way. In biological evolution, we know not only that there are mutations, but also, more importantly, that sexual reproduction leads to the production of offspring which are not exact copies of either of their parents. The genetic mechanism is precisely such that a large range of possibilities is explored, spread out over time from any pure condition. Physical constraints mean that some behaviours do better than others, and so there is a differential rate of survival and of reproduction. If possibility space is seen as a kind of 'evolutionary landscape', with hills representing behaviours of high performance, then simulations lead to the amplification of populations which are higher on the hill, and the suppression of those which are lower down.

For example Figure 2.3 demonstrates how in 'possibility space', an initially pure population will diffuse outwards as a result of sexual reproduction, mutations and entropic processes. As this takes place differential success makes it climb hills. In the studies referred to above the initial papers showed how the imperfect reproduction of populations provided a capacity to climb the hills of the adaptive landscape. By defining populations with different intensities of 'error-making' or 'imperfect reproduction', it was possible to identify the 'best' amount to ascend a given slope. Evolution was shown to select for populations with the ability to learn, rather than for populations with optimal behaviour. This corresponds to the selection of 'diversity-creating' mechanisms in the behaviour of populations, initially involving genetics, and later cognitive processes.

Figure 2.3   The co-evolution of performance and possibility space

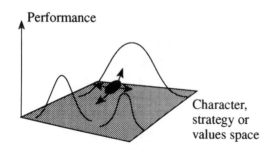

Performance

Character,
strategy or
values space

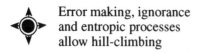

Error making, ignorance
and entropic processes
allow hill-climbing

   Such a view of evolution allows us to understand how it was that 'Neo-
Darwinism' came to resemble the old ideas of equilibrium physics. Neo-
Darwinists assumed that if a population had managed to get to the top of a
hill then this demonstrated their 'fitness'. In fact for such a population it
was advantageous to suppress 'error-making' and imperfect reproduction.
Evolution was 'over' since there was nowhere better to evolve to, and
nothing to learn. If this were the case, however, the final state of the system
could have been predicted. It would mark the inevitable end point of
evolution, and the 'equilibrium' solution. However of course, this view is
false because the shape of the hills in possibility space reflects the
populations that happen to be present. In other words, the advantage to be
gained from a particular behaviour depends on what other behaviours are
present at the time. The hills, and the populations co-evolve.
   Allen and McGlade (1987a) have conducted a series of experiments on
the evolutionary drive. What these tend to show is that this mixture of
exploratory diffusion of individuals in some behaviour space, and their
differential successes, makes the difference between what is 'organic' and
what is merely 'mechanical'.   There is a process of simultaneous
'stretching' and 'squeezing' (see Figures 2.4a and 2.4b) of populations in
the space of possible behaviours that is the core of our new understanding.
In further computer experiments it was also shown formally that if some
characteristic or strategy could exist which would result in self-
reinforcement, then once it had emerged it could trap the population and
block evolution at least for some time. An example of this from biology is
the 'Peacock's tail', where a gene produces the beautiful tail in the male,

and makes such a tail attractive to the female. In sexual reproduction, anything which enhances the probability of mating produces a positive feedback on its own population dynamics, and fixes itself. However, it is sometimes at the expense of functionality with respect of the external environment. Peacocks' tails are not an aid to finding their food better, or escaping predators, but simply the mark of a positive feedback trap.

Figure 2.4a   Stretching and squeezing

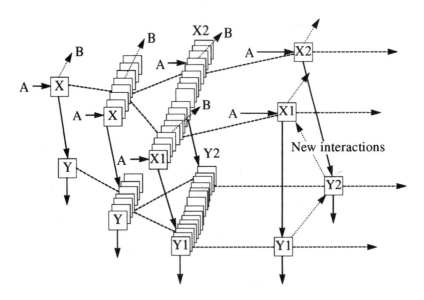

In human systems, such positive feedback systems abound. Indeed much of culture can be defined as behaviour which is fixed in this way. In most situations imitative strategies cannot easily be eliminated by an evolutionary process, and so fashions, styles and indeed whole cultures rise and decline without necessarily expressing any clear functional advantages. In this sense 'culture' may be viewed not so much as being 'the best' way of doing things somewhere, but perhaps as resulting from ignorance of other ways of doing things. Human activities in general, from fishery science to Patagonian folk dance, from modern economics 'professionalism' to traditional 'rites of passage' in primitive societies, exhibit these properties of autocatalytic, self-organisation, where ritual and shared ideology emerge and serve as the identity and focus of a social group, irrespective of the precise merits or indeed 'truth' of the ideology itself. It is in this way that so much of human attention is focused on playing a role in groups where values are generated internally and where the physical world outside is largely irrelevant.

Figure 2.4b   Evolution and speciation

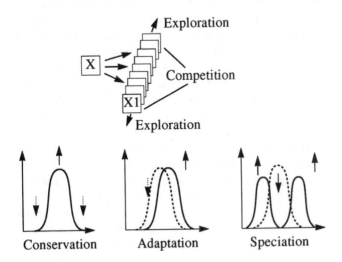

The work described above has been further extended to show how 'adaptive landscapes' are not exogenous but are actually generated by the mutual interaction of populations (Allen and Phang, 1993). In the space of 'possibilities' it is closely similar populations that are most in competition with each other, since they feed off the same resources, and suffer from the same predators. At the same time there is some 'distance' in character space, some level of dissimilarity, at which the two populations do not compete with each other. Consider initially a homogeneous population that grows until it reaches the limits set by the competition for underlying resources. At this point, there is a positive payoff for error makers, who escape somewhat from competition. We could say that although initially there was no 'hill' to climb, the population effectively digs a valley for itself, until there is a 'hill' to climb on either side of the present character 'centroid'. However, over some distance in this space population growth is restricted because of the 'competitive shadow' of the original population, and so populations diffuse in small numbers up the slope away from the original type.

After a certain time, however, small populations arise which are sufficiently different from the original type that they can grow and multiply on the basis of some other resource. In turn, one of these new populations may increase until it too is limited by internal competition for the limiting resource, and once again there is a payoff for deviants, particularly for those on the outside of the distribution, as they climb another self-made hill towards unpopulated regions of character space. In this way, well-defined populations appear successively, and colonists diffuse out from each of them as they reach a competitive limit, gradually filling character space with a set of populations separated approximately by some distance which is characteristic of the resource diversity which can be tapped.

From a single population our model generates a simple ecology, and a dynamic one since the identity of each population is maintained by the balance between a continual diffusion of deviants outwards into character space, and the differential reproduction and survival that is due to the presence of the other populations. Random events which occur during the 'filling' process will affect which populations arise, and so it is not true that the evolution represents the discovery of pre-existing 'niches'. On the contrary such a system operates beyond the mechanical paradigm, because its response to external interventions can involve changes in structure and of the 'identity' of the populations in the system. Harvesting particular populations in such a system, as in fishing for example, will provoke a complex response from the other populations (Allen and McGlade, 1987b). The identity of each species depends on that of the others, and on the accidents of its particular history. Removing, or severely depleting one or several populations, will therefore set in motion a series of responses, and changes in behaviour of other species which may look very like (and indeed be) a form of learning. Deviant behaviour which hitherto encountered a negative payoff may instead be reinforced, and in addition the responses may be essentially unpredictable. Figure 2.5 provides an illustration of the working of such an evolutionary process leading to the emergence of an 'ecology'. It may be seen that the identities of the populations are interdependent, and the response to any perturbation is more than merely mechanical.

In other words evolution is more than just the conversion of energy and matter in order to maintain the individuals of populations. It is the process through which populations compete, cooperate and co-evolve. They do so through a process of error-making whereby those who succeed are best able to survive in a constantly shifting ecological landscape. In each case a population's ecology is changing as a result of the behaviour of all other populations in that environment. There is no such thing as equilibrium since the wider system (the environment) is continually in a state of flux and change. Because of this our capacity to predict the future behaviour of ecologies is weak.

Figure 2.5   The emergence of an ecology

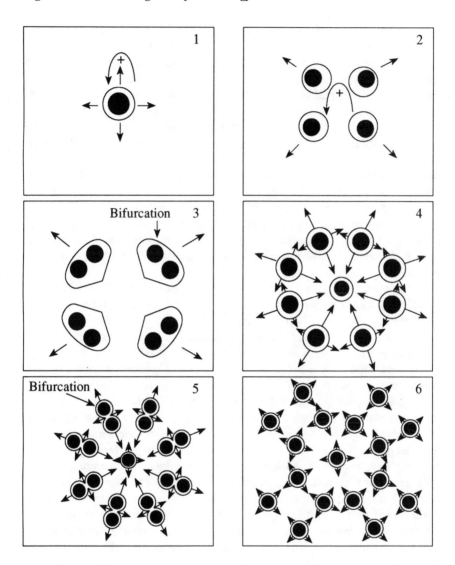

2.8   COMPLEXITY

Let us now examine the question of complexity in a little more detail by making a contrast with physics. It is arguable that the success of physics over the past centuries really resulted from the limits that it set on its ambitions. Firstly, physics set out to discover how things worked, rather than why they existed,[5] and in addition it avoided the problem of the origin and evolution of complex systems. By complex systems, we mean systems which have evolved a hierarchy of functional structure. For example, a tree is made of different parts – for example, trunk, roots, leaves – and each of these is composed of certain types of cell, arranged in an appropriate structure for its function, and the different types of cell are composed of membranes, cellular fluids, nuclei and so on. The whole system is maintained by flows of nutrients, which are captured, channelled and broken down in such a way as to maintain, and even augment the tree. Clearly, all living organisms are characterised by complexity, as are the results of their collective interactions, as in cities, and social and economic systems.

As systems evolve they usually do so in the direction of increasing complexity. By this we mean not only that the number of participating components of the system increases but also that the pattern of interrelationships amongst these components is also becoming more elaborate – that is, their number and type is increasing. For example, a given landscape may be capable of supporting greater numbers of its constituent populations who proceed to expand over time. However, in any given population some members are more successful than others. Perhaps these differentiate from their fellows and establish a new 'niche' in which their competitive and symbiotic relations with other populations become qualitatively different. The evidence from biological systems is that this certainly happens as their ecology becomes more 'mature', but not nearly to such an extent as with socio-economic systems. The last two to three centuries have seen an explosion of demographic and economic activity unparalleled in history. It is precisely the effects of this explosion which are now beginning to cause real concern since the capacity of the wider (world) environment to cope with it is being increasingly called in question. We shall explore the phenomenon of increasing complexity of human systems later in the text but at this stage it is useful to highlight economic complexity.

In the Middle Ages and well into the nineteenth century economic systems were much simpler than they are now. The bulk of populations lived and worked in a setting of subsistence agriculture, communications were poor, technology primitive and there was little in the way of industrial activity. What the Industrial Revolution did for Britain (and later for

Western Europe, Japan and the USA) was to set in train a process of economic differentiation which altered dramatically not only the capacity to create wealth but also the sheer number of economic agents (households, firms etc.) and their interrelationships. The growth of a capital goods sector increased the 'roundaboutness' of economic production which in turn placed a premium upon transport and communications of goods and services. More significantly perhaps, much of the new industry depended upon technological improvements which brought along with them the need for communications of a different sort – that of information.

By the beginning of the twentieth century this search for (and processing of) information was starting to become institutionalised in research and development (R&D) laboratories located both within the productive sector itself (as part of firms) and as part of the public sector (supported and maintained by government departments and ministries). Nowadays it is probably correct to claim that physical flows of commodities are now taking second place to information flows in economic intercourse such that the evolution of economic systems depends, in a fundamental sense, upon patterns of information access, storage, processing and diffusion (Clark and Juma, 1992).

While it is actually quite difficult to capture these ideas of evolutionary complexity as applied to economic systems, the following discussion may prove helpful. One of the earliest development economists to explore long-term structural change was Celso Furtado (1971) and we have used his book *Development and Underdevelopment* as the basis for the following account.[6] If we consider the early medieval European economy we can imagine it both spatially and economically as quite simple and stable. Economic production took place in isolated settlements (Figure 2.6, A&B) while the range of commodities produced and the technologies used were primitive indeed. Gradually, however, the impact of trade (and associated political conquest) began to increase the *spatial interrelatedness* of these settlements, bringing with it an accompanying increase in the volume and heterogeneity of consumer goods and expanding the spatial extent of economic production as a whole (Figure 2.6, C). Furtado calls this process one of 'agglutination' and suggests that it played an essential enabling role in the subsequent evolution of the international economy.

Economic activity began to spread across the available space almost like a rash does on the body of a diseased patient, transforming irreversibly both the texture of the landscape and the lives and livelihoods of succeeding generations. Spatial evolution by itself, however, could never have been the end of the story simply because the capacity to increase economic production by means of extensive trade and specialisation began to run into problems of increasing costs. It became simply too expensive, and too risky,

Figure 2.6   Progressive economic differentiation

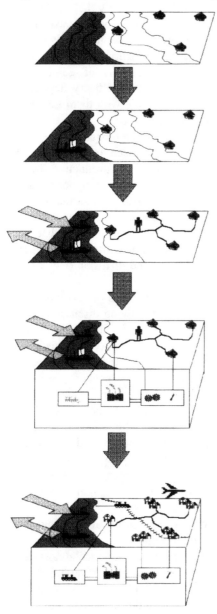

to continue to build bigger ships and to undertake longer and more dangerous voyages in the pursuit of economic gain. Sooner or later an alternative avenue for human creativity had to be found and that, as we now know, was the avenue of *economic differentiation* based upon, and itself promoting, the use of new and better technology. This phenomenon has also been labelled *development in depth* to distinguish it from the *development in breadth* that characterised the earlier epoch. As we mentioned above complexity began slowly also to take the form of increasing the roundaboutness of economic production. Commodities were no longer produced solely by the craftsman but began also to be produced in factories under controlled conditions (Figure 2.6, D&E).

An important element in these changes was that of *economic specialisation* (sometimes called the division of labour) whereby production processes began increasingly to concentrate on particular types and patterns, with an accompanying differentation of skills, machinery and related technology (Figure 2.7). As Rosenberg points out in his analysis of nineteenth-century United States growth,[7] for example, industrialisation was characterised by the emergence of a capital goods sector that 'specialised' in the production of the different kinds of tools and other machinery required for the eventual manufacture of goods and services finally sold to the consumer – for example, textiles machinery to make the looms, to weave the cloth, to be sold on to the dyer and the garment maker, and so on. And it was the technological dynamism of this machinery-producing sector itself that permitted economic creativity to reach new, hitherto unheard of, heights of productive performance.

The division of labour that has accompanied the industrialisation process has not only dramatically increased economic complexity, it has also had marked effects on the degree of instability of economic systems as well as their rate of structural change, effects that have accelerated rapidly throughout the twentieth century. Thus whereas economic systems could be considered as relatively simple, even as late as the beginning of the twentieth century – i.e. in the sense that their parameters remained fairly stable over reasonably long time periods – this is certainly no longer the case. Nowadays the impact of information technology and other 'globalisation' processes are such that structural change occurs at a much more rapid rate. And it is for this reason that the need to orchestrate events has become so much more crucial. Economic complexity has now reached a stage where change, and often irreversible change, requires a degree of monitoring and control that was simply unnecessary in previous epochs.[8] And, as we go on to stress in Chapter 6, such 'management' will certainly also require the development and use of decision tools that themselves can handle the evolutionary process.

Figure 2.7   The division of labour

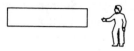

One worker performs all operations

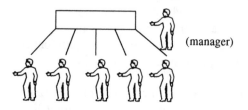

(manager)

Division of labour takes place. Each worker specialises. Productivity increases (tools)

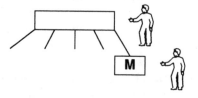

Machines invented to improve labour power

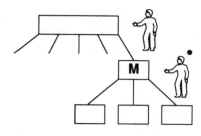

Technological improvement to machines takes place. More roundabout production within the firm

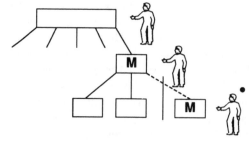

Firms begin to spin off and sell to other firms. Economic systems become more complex

● = Entrepreneur

The final point to make about increasing economic complexity concerns environmental planning. As economic systems evolve towards the end of the twentieth century it is becoming increasingly clear that uncontrolled evolution is likely to have damaging environmental consequences. It is also clear, however, that unless we fully understand the real behaviour of economic systems, attempts to modify their evolution may actually lead to worse outcomes. The paradox is that as economic behaviour is becoming more complex so also it is becoming more opaque, and hence the danger of 'mis-diagnosis' is growing at precisely the time when our forecasts need to be correct. The following chapters will explore this problem in more detail. For example, we shall argue that conventional planning techniques rest upon a 'simple systems' metaphor – i.e. that economic systems are depicted as *mechanisms*, an understanding of whose functioning allows us to alter their behaviour in (supposedly) beneficial ways. However, since in reality we are dealing with complex systems, there is a need for planning methods and decision tools which take complexity into account.

2.9   THE SCIENTIFIC METHOD

Finally it is important to recognise that understanding systemic creativity requires a qualitative shift in our grasp of what science is. The basis of scientific understanding has traditionally been the mechanical model (Rosen, 1974, 1987). In this view, the behaviour of a system can be understood, and anticipated, by classifying and identifying its components and the causal links, or mechanisms, that act between them. In physical systems, the fundamental laws of nature such as the conservation of mass, momentum and energy govern these mechanisms, and determine entirely what must happen.

By isolating or closing a system so that no new matter or energy can flow in to disturb it, such limits are placed on possible behaviour that classical physics was able to predict the properties of the final state quite generally for almost any physical system, however complex. The final state was that of thermodynamic equilibrium, and the properties of matter that would characterise it could be calculated in a very wide range of problems. This was such a triumph for classical science, that it was believed (erroneously) that analogous ideas must apply in the domains of biology, ecology and the human sciences.

But such ideas were misguided. In fact systems encountered in, for example, ecology and economics are always open to flows of matter and energy, and only attain thermodynamic equilibrium with death. Ironically mathematics, and related methods borrowed from 'all-conquering' physics and applied to the living world, have largely been inappropriate. For living systems are in constant dialogue (not equilibrium) with their environment, and even when not visibly evolving, maintain the capacity to evolve and change which is related to their underlying diversity. Although biological, ecological or human systems are discussed in terms of the typical behaviour of typical elements, or stereotypes, that make up the classification scheme that has been decided upon, *underneath* any such scheme there is always the greater particularity and diversity of reality.

In the classical scientific view, the future of a system is predicted by the simple expedient of considering the behaviour of the equations which govern its motion. Explanation in this case is reduced to an illumination of *how a system functions, but not to why the system has become what it is.* But while it is easy to write down the equations of mechanics for imaginary point particles, when considering a real system it is always necessary to make approximations in order to arrive at the mechanical equations which are supposed to govern its motion. The assumption that must be made is that the elements making up the variables (individuals within a population, firms in a sector etc.) are *all* identically that of the average type, in which case, the model reduces to a 'machine' which represents the system in terms of a set of differential (perhaps even non-linear) equations which govern its variables. This is the Newtonian vision of the world as a vast and complex clockwork mechanism.

Under this view, predictions are made by simply running the model forward in time, so that statements about the future, under given conditions, can be made by studying the types of solution that are possible for the equations in the long term. Scientific explanation of this kind is based on the inevitability of its final state. The idea of 'equilibrium' comes from the simplistic assumption that there will only be a single solution of these equations – a point attractor – and therefore that whatever happens the systems will eventually finish up there. This 'point attractor' solution of the differential equations is viewed as expressing a maximum or minimum of some potential function, just as in physics the dissipative forces of friction and viscosity act so as to lead any mechanical system towards a thermodynamic equilibrium expressing maximum entropy. But this is completely false for open systems.

Even in systems which we would all agree are purely physical, when they become open to flows of energy and matter there is no longer necessarily a unique final state expressing some 'optimal' principle. Indeed we now know that systems of non-linear differential equations can have a whole multiplicity of possible solutions, from stationary homogeneous kinds, through chaotic, heterogeneous ones, to ordered spatial and temporal structures. The external experimental conditions therefore no longer suffice to determine a unique future, since such systems can structure in a variety of ways depending on the internal details of their constituent components –

details which cannot be controlled from the outside of the system.

In other words, there is a single, predictable outcome to experiments on isolated systems – thermodynamic equilibrium – but not for open systems where matter and/or energy can flow through the system. This changes profoundly both our notion of 'explanation', and of scientific understanding. When non-linear mechanisms are present, the system may continue to change indefinitely, either executing a cyclic path of some kind, or possibly even a chaotic movement around a 'strange attractor'. More importantly, its evolution may involve structural changes of spatial and hierarchical organisation, in which qualitatively different characteristics emerge and new problems, satisfactions and issues can be 'turned on' spontaneously by the system.

Figure 2.8 Reduction of the complex to the simple in mathematical modelling

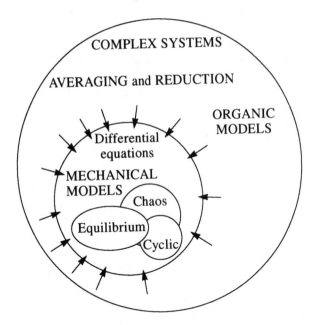

This capacity for structural change is not contained in the dynamical equations of conventionally described mechanical systems which are thus capable of functioning, but not of evolving. Rather, evolutionary change results from what has been 'removed' (in the reduction to the deterministic description) that is non-average. The system is therefore driven by two kinds of terms: deterministic average mechanisms operating between typical components, and non-average local behaviour that in non-linear systems can be amplified and lead to qualitative structural changes in the average mechanisms, a distinction we have tried to depict very roughly (and metaphorically) in Figure 2.8. What this diagram intends to show is that while reality is complex (represented by the outer circle) we tend progressively to simplify things in order to make reality amenable to simple mathematical models, ending up with the considerably reduced equilibrium models represented by the inner ellipse.   The scientific method, as conventionally understood, is capable of dealing with the latter, reduced, description but not with the former.

2.10 CONCLUSION AND SUMMARY

In this chapter we have provided a summary description of our own view of the nature of systems, making the following points.

1. Systems are 'whole' phenomena made up of interconnected elements. Their boundaries separate them from their environment and the pattern of relationship which any system has with its environment determines whether it is 'isolated', 'closed' or 'open'.
2. Living (organic) systems may be distinguished from non-living (physical) systems in so far as:
    (a) they are open;
    (b) their component elements are organised;
    (c) these elements are affected by their participation in systemic behaviour;
    (d) they (the systems) exhibit behaviour (while transforming inputs into outputs);
    (e) they also demonstrate resilience in the face of externally generated perturbation, particularly where they possess considerable species diversity.
3. Systemic description requires characterisation and definition of its constituent elements. There are two methods of doing this:
    (a) phenetic – counting characteristics of sufficiently similar elements or species;
    (b) cladism – identifying the evolutionary history of sufficiently similar elements or species.
4. Both types of taxonomy are difficult to use but (b) has the advantage that it introduces the notion of change. The study of how species within a system change through time is called population dynamics.
5. Populations (and therefore also the systems they inhabit) evolve not

according to mechanical laws of motion but rather through a process of complicated interactions with their environments, characterised by the seemingly spontaneous emergence of new forms/structures under conditions of uncertainty.

6. One way of exploring this 'evolutionary drive' behaviour has been the creation of simulated models of change in which populations randomly explore their environments (which themselves are continuously changing). Such simulated 'hill-climbing' experiments appear to show that evolution selects for populations with the ability to learn rather than those which slavishly follow fixed rules regardless of the context.

7. The complexity of a system defines the number and interconnectedness of its constituent elements. It also defines internal arrangements of hierarchy. As systems evolve they tend to increase in complexity but this is especially true of human systems. For example, the last two to three centuries may be seen historically as one of rapid growth of complexity on the part of economic systems in which interrelatedness is now becoming as much informational as it is mediated by flows of energy and matter.

8. Conventional scientific methodology is inadequate by itself to explain the behaviour of living systems since it is very much governed by mechanistic reasoning. Evolutionary change, however, requires a methodology that is non-deterministic and allows for non-average local behaviour.

NOTES

1 For a useful collection of some of the classic papers in this tradition see Emery (1970) which includes a paper by von Bertalanffy referencing some of his own early ones.
2 See Gell-Mann (1994), Chapter 3. We are grateful also to Sylvan Katz for drawing our attention to some of these points.
3 See Conway (1993), p. 52. See also Conway (1984) for an extensive treatment of this and related questions.
4 For a useful discussion on these issues see, for example, Ridley (1985).
5 Or at least it did so until the development of 'big bang' theories in recent years.
6 See also Clark (1985), Chapter 2, for a more detailed discussion of what follows.
7 See Rosenberg (1976), Chapter 1.
8 These and related aspects have been explored extensively by Clark and Juma (1992). See also Clark (1988).

3. Economic Systems

3.1 INTRODUCTION

Our aim in Chapter 2 was to define the concept of a 'system' and its generic properties independently of the context in which it is to be applied, and in particular to focus on evolutionary systems and how they typically behave. Our main purpose in doing this at an early stage in the book was to emphasise a range of homologous properties between natural systems and economic systems, properties that will become clearer as our argument progresses. In fact recent years have seen a gradual introduction of the application of systems thinking to innovation and socio-economic change. The characterisation of 'national systems of innovation', for example, by Freeman, Nelson and others[1] has been made at least in part to emphasise the interconnectedness but at the same time the separateness of institutions concerned with innovation. Since each such system is demonstrably different in a variety of respects it becomes interesting and useful to view each in systemic ways, the main aim being to discover what characteristics appear to make for greatest economic and technological success. From an analytical viewpoint, however, a major problem is to find the concept of a 'system' defined independently of the context in which it is being used. What precisely is an economic system? How does it differ from a 'production system' or an 'innovation system'? What are their respective component parts and what are their patterns of interrelationship? What properties do they possess which allow us to call them systems? And so on.

The purpose of this chapter is to define in as clear a way as possible the nature of economic systems and how they may be conceptualised in ways similar to generic systems outlined in the previous chapter. This is actually not an easy task to accomplish since the conventional means of describing economic systems (and how they behave) do not lend themselves readily to it. Indeed one of the major problems of economic systems, at least to our eyes, is that they are thought about in terms of the mechanical. They are machines. They do not evolve. For this reason our description of standard economic theory will of necessity be a critical one in this respect. Nevertheless the description has to be made since only against a backcloth

of prevailing practice can we begin to see clearly its problems and potential
alternative solutions.

3.2 ECONOMIC ANALYSIS

There are a variety of definitions of 'economics' but usually they have the
following two characteristics in common.

1. The subject is concerned with commodities (i.e. goods and services) and
   how these are produced, distributed and consumed.
2. It is concerned with the allocation of scarce resources amongst
   competing ends or goals.

The first introduces the notion of material things (which in some sense
are conducive to human welfare), while the second explores the efficiency
with which these (commodities) are produced, distributed and consumed.
Analysis proceeds by means of abstraction, that is, by a process through
which the analyst assumes away most of the complexities of human systems
in order to lay bare the essential relationships he wishes to focus on. In the
case of economics, analysis takes place by exploring two types of economic
system, namely the whole (or macro) economy and its component (or
micro) constituents.

Figure 3.1   The circular flow of income in the macroeconomy

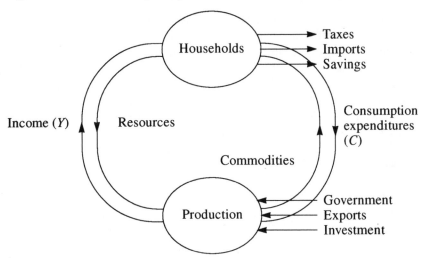

Let us start by examining the macroeconomy where economic space is conventionally divided up into two subsystems: (i) the production system (P) which transforms resources (inputs) into commodities (outputs) and (ii) the household system (H) which owns the means of production (natural resources, labour and capital), earns income from them by selling them to the production system and (finally) uses this income to purchase the commodities produced by that system. Where both the P and H sectors spend all their incomes (on consumption, C) accruing to them over a specific time period, the macro system is a closed one in which all resources are conserved. Graphically these relationships may be portrayed in terms of the well-known circular flow of income diagram (Figure 3.1) which is often then modified to include specific categories of 'systemic openness', namely foreign trade, government activity, and disturbance arising out of the behaviour of savers and investors.

In the first case households are taxed (T) and the state uses these resources to spend resources (G) on behalf of the consumer. In the second case households spend incomes on imports (M) which are of course produced by other (overseas) economic systems, and in order to pay for these our own economic system has to export (X) commodities of an equivalent aggregate value. In the third case households save (S) part of their incomes (Y) and these savings are used (via the capital market) for the purchase of investment goods (I) by the productive sector. Equilibrium is established where

$$Y + T + M + S = C + G + X + I \qquad (3.1)$$

but since the economic agents are not identical there is a constant tendency to instability mediated by negative feedback mechanisms (mainly price). The theory of macroeconomics is concerned largely with the determinants of economic behaviour on the part of the agents involved and with the conditions under which the macrosystem will achieve and maintain an equilibrium consistent with full utilisation of available resources. Where equilibrium does not obtain, macroeconomic analysis (and controversy) focuses on what measures need to be taken to re-achieve it.

The constituent elements of the H and P sectors (i.e. the individual households and firms) represent the 'microstates' of the wider macrosystem. As with the macroeconomy these are analysed in relation to their mutual interactions, that is, as exchanges of commodities and resources at prices which broadly reflect the forces of supply and demand. The economic study of these individual market relationships is called microeconomics and tells us how the market for any particular commodity (or resource) behaves, what properties it has and how efficiently it does its job. It also tells us something about the behaviour of the agents involved –

how much, for example, the firms in any specific industry are able to monopolise production and thereby raise prices above marginal costs of production. What economic analysis does not do, however, is to provide any direct insight into how the behaviour of microeconomic agents affects the macroeconomic context.

In particular there are important questions about how the (macro)economic system evolves. How, for example, does its capacity to produce goods and service increase? Or how does its structure change? How do new industries arise and how does new technology impinge on the economic fabric? The answer to these and many similar questions is, sadly, that the apparatus of economic analysis, at least in its pure (or 'mainstream') form, has little to say. It is instructive to speculate on why this should be so since it enables us to see clearly why much of the analytical strength of economic analysis is achieved at the expense of its capacity to handle economic change.

There are several factors involved here but probably the best place to start is to focus on two related features: (i) the underlying rationalism of the profession itself; (ii) the sharp analytical disjunction conventionally drawn between the microstates and the macrostates of any economic system. We shall not spend much time on the first, since it is a professional trait that has been extensively explored by ourselves and by many others in a variety of contexts.[2] What we would simply claim is that it rests upon a deeply rooted, and in our view often incompletely thought through, philosophical position regarding the nature of knowledge and how it may legitimately be sought. The second feature is also deeply embedded into the institutional and cognitive fabric of the profession. Moreover it (i.e. the relationship between the microstates and the macrostates of an economic system) is one that is seldom discussed in standard economic theory. Instead they are each discussed as separate systems tending towards equilibrium in the 'short period', that is in a time interval during which the capital stock does not vary.[3] Economic growth – the rate at which economic systems increase their capacity to produce commodities – does not arise as a direct theoretical result of microeconomic behaviour but is rather viewed entirely in macroeconomic terms. And this has been so right throughout the history of economic thought.[4]

Thus the classical economists (broadly speaking the tradition that prevailed up until the latter part of the nineteenth century) argued that aggregate growth depended upon aggregate investment – the production of goods and services not for immediate consumption but rather for commodities such as machines that would improve productivity. They also felt incidentally that possibilities for growth would ultimately be limited by diminishing returns such that each successive round of investment would become less and less productive, and eventually stagnation would ensue.

However, as the twentieth century progressed and it became clear that growth rates showed no signs of falling (in the industrialised countries they were increasing), stagnationist pessimism gave way to a new (but still macroeconomic) view that economic growth depended mainly on 'non-economic' factors. Pereira-Mendes (1991) puts the point neatly as follows. 'In equilibrium models of growth, it [was] "elegantly" demonstrated that the rate of economic growth was not dependent upon the propensity to save or the rate of profit (or any other economic variable ...) but solely upon the proportional rate of growth in the labour force and the Harrod – neutral rate of technical progress'.[5]

But what are these 'non-economic' factors which lead to 'technical progress'? And what is the mechanism through which they impinge upon economic production? The way this has been handled is by postulating a 'residual' or 'coefficient of ignorance' which describes the incapacity of economic analysis to explain growth. A series of empirical investigations in the 1950s and 1960s concluded (mainly for the United States) that depending upon the statistical assumptions made, this incapacity amounted to between 60% and 90% of observed economic growth – clearly a considerable level of ignorance. A somewhat embarrassed economics profession subsequently sought to 'explain' the residual by ascribing certain 'exogeneous' causes (like education for example). The best example of this genre, Denison, was the author of a series of statistical studies which attempted to disaggregate the residual into its constituent parts.[6] For example, in one study of the US economy between 1929 and 1957 (which grew by 2.93% per annum on average) Denison (1962) breaks down 2.00% (i.e. roughly two-thirds) into 0.43% (increase of capital stock), 0.58% ('advances in knowledge'), 0.12% (organised R&D expenditures) and 0.87% (educational improvements).

However, it is not clear why these various causal influences can be viewed as acting independently of each other (as they must if they are each to be given separate percentage values). It seems far more likely that they act together as part of a complex evolving whole. For example, increases in the capital stock usually embody 'advances in knowledge', require more 'educated' workers to man the new machines and involve a lot of trouble-shooting R&D (which itself brings about 'advances in knowledge'). But of course to make this point is simply to close off explanation at the macro level. Indeed it is probably not too unfair to suggest that the 'residual' would appear to have the same explanatory characteristics as the well-known 'placebo effect' in modern medicine.

Over the last ten to twenty years or so the neo-Schumpeterian school of economics has begun to take the   concept of economic change more seriously. The reason why they are called neo-Schumpeterians is that they all take inspiration from the Austrian economist Joseph Schumpeter who, in a series of books and papers in the first half of this century, sought to explain how economic systems grow. For Schumpeter, the inspiration for growth was *innovation* which he defined in terms of novelty – new products, new processes, new markets, new resources and new organisational forms. Innovations occurred as a result of 'entrepreneurial' behaviour on the part of business people who were in turn activated by competition and by the lure of monopoly profits. It was the entrepreneur who was the creative force driving the economic system on to greater heights of achievement. Provide conditions appropriate for entrepreneurship, and the economy would flourish.

Implicitly, therefore, although Schumpeter did not express it in this way, he was describing a process through which the macro evolves out of the micro. The collective behaviour of individual people in exploring 'economic possibility space' (to use the language of Chapter 2) would drive the economic system as a whole to ever new heights of productive possibility. It is this micro–macro interface that the neo-Schumpeterians have begun to explore. One of its most eminent exponents, Christopher Freeman, in a book first published in 1974, *The Economics of Industrial Innovation*, provided what is probably the first microeconomics of innovation text. In a series of case studies of science and technology (S/T) -based industries (chemicals, pharmaceuticals and electronics capital goods) he explored the nature of innovative behaviour at firm and sector level stressing the importance of the professionalised R&D laboratory, the complexity of many innovations, the uncertainty that surrounds their development, the heterogeneity of production inputs and relevant people-embodied skills. In so doing he has made a tremendous contribution to our understanding of economic dynamics by, in a sense, providing much needed empirical data on the actual details of what Schumpeter had originally described.

But since his work could not be readily assimilated into economic orthodoxy it has largely been ignored by the economics mainstream. For example, with reference to the issue of technological unemployment Soete (1986) wonders 'what the exact nature of the contribution of detailed innovation expertise and micro study could be [since such studies] ... through their inherent methodological failure in fully comprehending the various macroeconomic employment compensation mechanisms could be said to confuse rather than to clarify the issue'.[7] What this means is that the prevailing systemic dualism of the economics profession could not assimilate easily Freeman's results. But this has not deterred the neo-Schumpeterians who have now developed a considerable body of (mainly empirical) knowledge about economic innovation and change. Its characteristics are:

- the central importance of S/T expenditures;
- the firm-specific and cumulative nature of technical change knowledge;
- the importance of economic organisation;
- the role of institutions as mobilisers of innovation;
- the heterogeneity of relevant microeconomic behaviour;
- the central role of information, how it is accessed, processed, used and disseminated.

3.3   ECONOMIC SYSTEMS AS COMPLEX SYSTEMS

It is against this background that we return to the questions set out at the beginning of this chapter and in particular pose the question – how may we characterise economic systems in ways that are more consistent with the general properties of systems set out in the previous chapter? In another text[8] one of the authors of this book attempted to do this by using an analogy drawn directly from an entirely different field of study, that of early developmental psychology as portrayed by Arthur Koestler. In his book, *The Ghost in the Machine*, Koestler (1970) had set out a comprehensive critique of the (then) ruling mechanistic paradigm in psychology. His argument was that this paradigm, sometimes given the label 'behaviourism', failed to capture the richness of the human condition, with unfortunate implications for the kinds of social policies that were often given credence as a result. As an alternative he put forward a paradigm in which systems thinking played a major role and which he believed had homologous properties applicable to all facets of social organisation, including that of economics.

The essence of his argument, which is consistent with the generic properties of a 'system' outlined in Chapter 2, was that all natural systems, including social systems, may be described as *nested hierarchies*. Indeed it is this property that helps to define a system's 'structure' and its resultant 'functional' characteristics. For example, it will be recalled in Chapter 2 we defined a tree in precisely this way, that is, as comprising different parts (trunk, roots, leaves etc.) each of which is composed of certain types of cell and so on down the hierarchy. The whole system is maintained by flows of nutrients, which are captured, channelled and broken down in such a way as to maintain and propagate the functions of each of the tree's components.

Similarly a business firm is typically made up of a number of departments, each of which may be broken down into sub-units and then further subdivided, and so on. For example, the R&D department may be composed of a series of research programmes and each such programme may consist of a number of research projects. Both the firm and the tree, of course, are themselves part of larger systems. It was Koestler's view that all living systems display this property of hierarchy – often described as one of nested hierarchy, to bring home the idea that systems are nested inside each other, somewhat like the famous Russian Dolls. For this reason it should be obvious that it is normally not possible to act upon an individual component of a system without at the same time impinging upon the whole hierarchy with resultant impacts upon the system as a whole.

Koestler's hierarchies, however, are not rigid ones. They do not presuppose automatic relations of command and control as you move up and down the command structure. They are not 'army-like' in this traditional sense. This is because in order to function *in a creative way* each level of the hierarchy needs a certain amount of autonomous flexibility. What the higher level does is to provide the boundaries, or heuristic conditions, within which the next level down can operate, but these only describe the rules of the game. Within these 'rules' the next level down requires the freedom to alter its behaviour to meet unexpected circumstances/events that cannot be predicted. Indeed most modern systems theorists now agree that it is this property of systemic behaviour which allows natural systems to cope with indeterminacy, and hence distinguishes them from the more rigid mechanical arrangements that characterise *physical systems* – systems that are essentially uncreative.

A final point stressed by Koestler's analysis is that different hierarchical 'lineages' do not function independently of their neighbours. They interact on a variety of different levels to produce evolutionary outcomes of great complexity. These are sometimes described nowadays as 'associative nets' or 'networks' and are seen to play a significant role in the behaviour of the system as a whole.

> Hierarchies do not operate in a vacuum, but interact with others. This elementary fact has given rise to much confusion. If you look at a well-kept hedge surrounding a garden like a living wall, the rich foliage of the entwined branches form horizontal networks at numerous levels. Without the individual plants there would be no network. Without the network, each plant would be isolated, and there would be no hedge. 'Arborisation' and 'reticulation' (net-formation) are complementary principles in the architecture of organisms and societies. Thus the circulatory system controlled by the heart and the respiratory system controlled by the lungs function as quasi-autonomous, self-regulating hierarchies, but they interact on various levels. In the subject-catalogues in our libraries the branches are entwined through cross-references. In cognitive hierarchies – universes of discourse – arborisation is reflected in the 'vertical' denotation (classification) of concepts, reticulation in their 'horizontal' connotations in associative nets.[9]

How then can we apply these ideas to economic systems? The problem is that this is actually not very easy within conventional modes of thought since, as we have seen at the beginning of the chapter, economic systems are normally described in terms of the (simple) interaction of two subsystems – households and firms. And it is difficult to see how these two subsystems could meaningfully be analysed in terms of nested hierarchy. However, a useful starting point is to ignore the household sector altogether and to view the typical economy as merely a productive system, a procedure implicitly adopted by many analysts.

Thus we may view any economy as a specific entity, one of a number of economic systems within the world economy. It is governed by a set of rules (laws, customs, etc.) which lay the ground-plan (or 'macroeconomic context') for the various sectors which go to make it up. We can also say that each sector may in turn be split up into a variety of industrial 'types' (electronics, textiles, food, etc.) which each consist of a range of 'firms' defined as legal entities in economic space whose function it is to undertake the productive act. Again, each firm is itself made up of various components, which we may classify as 'divisions' each of which has a degree of autonomy within some overall corporate policy laid down at the centre. Finally, the divisions are themselves often subdivided into smaller units, or departments, in order to facilitate efficient operations.[10]

Figure 3.2   The macroeconomic system as a nested hierarchy

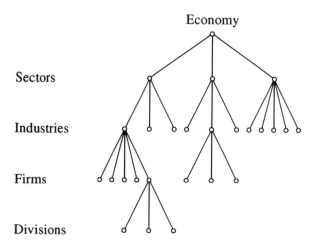

Hence conceived vertically (see Figure 3.2) the economic system is composed of layers of increasing detail as we proceed from the 'macro' (at the top) to the 'micro' (at the bottom). Intermediate layers are often labelled as 'meso' but are not give much prominence in economic analysis, mainly because their components are held not to have 'intent' – they do not operate as economic agents. Nor do they possess legal status. However, this is actually a considerable oversimplification. Industries, for example, are often organised into representative bodies which have considerable customary and legal jurisdiction over their members' behaviour. Similarly, government-sponsored regulatory bodies play an increasingly important role in the operations of most facets of the modern economy, and, as we outline below, there are nowadays a whole range of ancillary organisations which have become crucial to international economic competitiveness. Indeed there are some modern political theorists like Cawson (1985, 1986) who argue that such 'corporate' interests now play a major role in processes of policy making and execution under modern capitalism.

On the horizontal plane economic units interrelate through exchange of resources and information. The exchange of resources (i.e. commodities, factors of production and energy) amongst firms has traditionally formed the main agenda of microeconomic analysis, so that the 'firm' level has been the focus of attention. More recently, however, this exclusive focus has begun to be broken down in a number of respects but mainly because of the growing importance of information flows in economic intercourse, among which those relating to science and technology are by far the most important. For example, the growth of pre-competitive research clubs (whose membership consists of otherwise competing firms) is becoming increasingly strong. Sometimes these clubs are supported by state finance but their rationale includes the high costs of much modern R&D, the growing science-based nature of economic production and the realisation that putting resources into the information search process does not necessarily compromise competitive advantage.[11]

Another example is the development of temporary consortia or 'constellations' of firms for a specific productive task in order to mobilise complementary capabilities. This can be illustrated by the well-known Keiretsu system in Japan where (like in the automobile case) the 'productive unit' for a particular design of car is often a complicated arrangement of assembler, satellite component makers, distributers and sources of finance. Where another car is produced these arrangements may well lead to new recombinations. Indeed, there is now considerable evidence of technical changes occurring alongside shifting boundaries through merger, joint venture, subcontracting and other organisational devices across a wide range of modern industry production, as firms vie with each other to attain competitive advantage (Figure 3.3).[12]

Figure 3.3   Shifting forms of economic organisation in the car industry

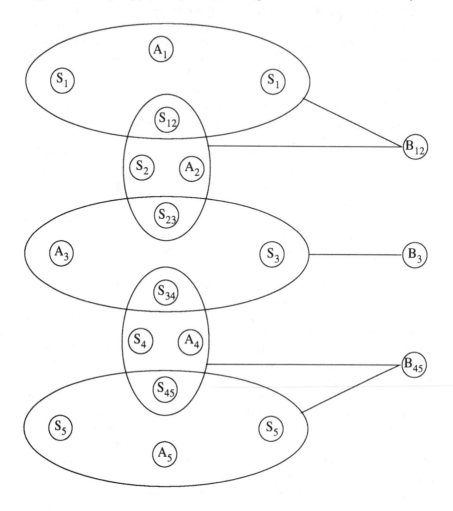

Notes:
Subscripts refer to relevant model of car.
A = Assembly firms
B = Banks
S = Subcontractors/supply firms

It may easily be seen, therefore, that even considering economic systems
just as productive systems, they clearly exhibit a degree of complexity of a
high order indeed. We defined complexity (in Chapter 2) in terms of the

number and intensity of the interrelationships amongst component parts of a system. Where economies are concerned, complexity is therefore a close function of the degree of 'roundaboutness' that is observed in economic production (and distribution), a feature of the modern economy that has been accelerating over recent decades. The so-called 'globalisation' of the international economy is perhaps the most obvious example of this trend (cf., for example, the growing dominance of multinational companies (MNCs) which by definition belong to more than one macroeconomy). However, economic differentiation is also increasing at lower levels as well. Thus, many firms (conglomerates) produce products from more than one (conventionally described) industrial sector, while within firms there are also often complicated cross-divisional linkages like, for example, where a common R&D department services several operational divisions.

For these reasons, then, it may easily be seen that in principle at least the notion of economic systems as analogous to other forms of 'system', in the sense described by Koestler, is not at all far-fetched. The idea of a hierarchy constraining lower-level behaviour is clearly present, as is the presence of complicated networking arrangements across different vertical strands of the productive system. Indeed we might even go so far as to argue that the pace of change of modern economic life is such that it is doubtful if economic production could proceed at all were it not for the growing proliferation of complicated networking arrangements across different components of the economic system.

3.4 TECHNOLOGICAL SYSTEMS AND EVOLUTIONARY BEHAVIOUR

So far in this chapter we have set out two propositions.

1. That standard economic theory has great difficulty coping with the phenomenon of structural change and that this is closely connected with deeply (and probably also subconsciously) held philosophical values. It is also related to its practice of separating analysis into two systems of enquiry without adequate interconnection between them.
2. That an alternative metaphor may prove more useful (namely one with the properties that have been outlined in the previous chapter), although it is clear that the systems analogy is by no means a straightforward one.

We have outlined both how this metaphor appears to fit in with neo-Schumpeterian views of economic change and how at a first approximation, principles of nested hierarchy may be applied to the description of the productive parts of economic systems. The next step is to establish the 'mechanics' of change – that is, to work out in some detail how economic evolution actually occurs. We emphasise this point simply because it is insufficient to put everything down to 'competition' in some general sense. That is rather like attributing the success of the modern battleship to Archimedes' principle. It is the richness of this competitive process that we ought now to begin to capture in our models. Here it is useful to return to the point made earlier in this chapter where we emphasised the role of technological change in economic growth.

In the Schumpeterian sense technological change has its roots in novelty in the production process.[13] And novelty arises as a result of investment in change which in turn can occur in many different ways – e.g. the purchase of new machinery, the training of staff, the hiring of new staff, the purchase of a patent, the construction of a new plant, the reorganisation of existing facilities, R&D expenditures, and so on. A convenient means of expressing the concept is that any one productive agent (say a firm) operates with a specific 'technological system' which is peculiar to its own operations and which in a sense encapsulates the knowledge necessary for production to be maintained. Such a system defines and orchestrates the range of competences that the firm possesses and summarises the economic efficiency with which it converts inputs into outputs. Another way of looking at the same phenomenon is as the information which a firm possesses contextualised into routines, work schedules, machinery, management control systems, production programmes and people-embodied skills which together underlie the production process as a whole at any point in time.

But this technological system is at the same time the focus of change because of economic competition from other firms that threaten to take away market share and reduce its profits. In addition creative forces within the firm have a similar effect in bringing about change. In this way the firm's technological system is perpetually in a state of flux (at least potentially) due to environmental competitive and internal creativity. In order to 'manage change' firms establish specific institutional mechanisms within which they focus resources and attempt to control events in a reasonably ordered way, since clearly continuous change would lead to great inefficiency. The most important such mechanism is the R&D laboratory, but it is not the only one. Examples of others are the dedicated 'project team' set up to engineer a new investment project, personnel appraisal schemes designed to improve manpower efficiency and periodic buying in of external management consultancy services.[14]

Nevertheless it is often convenient to focus on the R&D laboratory because in a sense it encapsulates most of the important features of technological change. Not only does it create the possibilities for competitive growth through the development of new products and processes. It also provides a window on external technological developments of potential relevance taking place within the wider technological system belonging to the economy as a whole (and indeed to other economies). By this we mean that in order to capture the significance of the vast amount of potentially relevant knowledge that is continuously being created, the firm needs to be conducting its own R&D at the same time.[15] This wider technological system has two aspects to it – a *geographical* (or *spatial*) aspect on the one hand and a *cognitive* (or *paradigmatic*) aspect on the other. Let us start with the latter since it has received extensive treatment by neo-Schumpeterian economists in recent years and because, though hard to define, it has important theoretical properties. The notion of the 'paradigm', initially credited to the science historian Thomas Kuhn, was first applied to technology by Constant in the early 1970s[16] in his study of the history of the jet engine. It has since been explored and elaborated by others and has come to be defined as that set of equipment and accompanying know-how which in a broad sense represents best practice for any given industry.

For example, transistor technology provided the basis for radically new and cheaper products throughout the 1950s and 1960s using the molecular structure of certain chemical elements as a channel for electronic signals which was markedly superior in many economic and technical respects to the older valve-based technology, which had gradually become increasingly clumsy and costly when incorporated in sequential forms of production. In terms of its 'productive evolution', valve technology had reached a dead end and the techno-economic response was to retrace the technology to first principles, as it were, and to strike off in a new direction.

In this case the basic principles – the set of scientific and technological principles which underlie the conversion of electrical power to artefacts which provide a range of services to the consumer – remained substantially the same. But the use of the transistor provided a means of reducing unit costs, size and bulkiness, and of improving the applicability of these artefacts to further areas of economic production. It thus represented a new technological paradigm for electronics industry in the post-war period.

However, the 'technological paradigm' is more than just the core technology (or 'dominant design' as some others have called it).[17] It is also a metaphor for a complex set of techno-economic relationships which are all part of the technology viewed as a 'system'. For example, in his analysis of the jet engine, Constant shows that this new paradigm had implications for the whole range of interindustry linkages associated with aircraft production (including links with consumers). When it replaced the older propellor-based technology, the jet engine revolution meant concomitant changes for airports, regulatory authorities, town planners, engine designers and manufacturers, airframe constructors, research laboratories, government departments, subcontractors, airlines and a host of related economic 'actors'.

The technological paradigm or system, therefore, represents a set of standard practices for production embodied in the skills and competences of relevant people and organisations. It is often science based and enshrined in specific engineering standards and codes of conduct which prescribe best practice. And in a dynamic sense it embodies strong prescription on the directions of technical change to pursue and those to neglect. In short it describes a technological system in 'cognitive space' providing the ruling heuristic for good technological practice.

The second aspect to the idea of a technological system is spatial – and to some extent also institutional. Here the phrase used is the science/technology (S/T) system since increasingly economic production depends upon basic as well as applied research and development to underpin its activities. Again the best-known organisational focus of this type is the R&D laboratory attached to the firm, but most modern economic systems possess a wide variety of institutions like government laboratories, semi-public research associations, institutes of testing and standards, specialist R&D companies, higher education bodies, consultancy companies and other similar bodies. Not all such organisations lie wholly within either the private or the public sector. In some cases, as we have mentioned, temporary consortia are put together for particular projects. In others, research clubs with company memberships are often established for pre-competitive research purposes where the companies concerned are actually in competition with each other. In general, modern productive enterprises in any industry have access to a wide variety of S/T sources which together can be said to comprise the 'technology system' for that industry.

Returning now to our artificial economy, we can say that for any given product a representative firm may be viewed as behaving within the constraints laid down by its industry of primary relevance. This involves (1) legal constraints (e.g. law pertaining to firm behaviour as laid down by government, (2) customary constraints (informal sanctions laid down by tradition), (3) technological constraints (those relating to the ruling technological system in vogue) and (4) economic constraints (e.g. market structure). What microeconomic analysis conventionally does is to describe a set of interrelationships under these circumstances, with a firm attempting to maximise (or optimise) some objectives' function in relation to a limited range of variables.

From our viewpoint, however, the industry is akin to the *species* where the classification is based upon similar product types. Competition is intraspecific such that any one firm is constantly aware of threats coming from rivals any or all of whom may be in a position to capture its markets (or a share of its markets) through a variety of courses of action (of which technological change represents a very important category but not the only one). This being the case it will normally take care to alter its own environment in such a way as to reduce the threat to itself, through such mechanisms as advertising, investment in R&D, control over factor supplies, taking over rivals, and so on. Where all firms are behaving similarly – at least within the overall framework provided by our representative economy – we have a situation of constant flux in which the environment is constantly changing in unpredictable ways. All that any one firm can reasonably do is to make sure that it remains abreast with what is happening and maintains the capacity to react quickly if things go wrong. Life is inherently and unavoidably uncertain. Determinate outcomes are certainly not the order of the day in a system which has a high degree of vulnerability like this one.

The evolutionary drive, therefore, takes place as part of the competitive process. Competitive firms explore their 'possibility space' by investing in what we may call technological change, that is, improving the overall productivity of their operations in ways summarised by Schumpeter and his followers. Not all succeed but those who do experience considerable gains in profitability and growth. Conversely the unsuccessful firms eventually die. The analogy with the more general evolutionary drive behaviour is clearly close. As the market in any area (or hill) of economic space becomes more congested some firms begin to explore new possibilities. Many fail, but some succeed in establishing a new 'niche'. Trail blazers are then followed by imitators who 'swarm' after them developing and then colonising a new area of economic space which will in its own turn become congested – and so on in an endless cycle of evolution.

Nothing could be further from the conventional nostrums of standard economic theory. Instead of predetermined equilibrium we have continuous (relative) instability. Instead of certainty we have uncertainty. And, most important of all, instead of artificial separation of 'micro' and 'macro' states on the vertical plane, we have a nested hierarchy of relationships whereby the macro evolves out of the micro as a necessary consequence of the competitive process and of cooperative relationships at lower levels of the hierarchy. Such a hierarchy is very complex since complicated networks of relationships emerge horizontally as part of the process of change. Nevertheless it is this complexity that is the reality around us and which our models should therefore really reflect.

3.5   SOME RECENT ISSUES

As we mentioned at the beginning of this chapter, however, the idea of seeing economic production in systemic terms is actually becoming much more common than it used to be. One good example of this trend is that of Miller and his colleagues who have recently been investigating innovation in what they describe as 'complex systems' industries. By this they appear to mean industries that do not produce homogeneous products that are sold directly to consumers but rather large-scale capital-intensive products which provide complicated arrays of services to downstream sectors. For Miller et al. (1995) the notion of a complex system 'describes a group of large scale, customised, engineering-intensive products, including flight simulators, telecommuni-cations exchanges, trains, ships, military systems, airplanes and electrical equipment. Complex systems exhibit emerging properties through time as they respond to the evolving needs of large users',[18] such as governments, for example.

Such industries are to be distinguished from other (presumably non-complex) industries in so far as the latter group cater for the mass market. Moreover the differences are most clearly seen with respect to innovative behaviour where 'complex systems' industries do not evolve in ways similar to those we described in the previous section but rather exhibit a kind of managed change influenced as much by institutional and regulatory factors as by the forces of competition. Indeed cooperation is an important feature of observed innovations in the case study the authors choose to try to demonstrate their point, that of flight simulators. For this group of researchers, then, the notion of a 'complex system' has got a lot to do with the complicated nature of the array of actors involved directly and indirectly with the provision of the ultimate service to the buyer.

Although we have no quarrel with the central message of the paper itself – i.e. that such industries can be objectively distinguished and can often show peculiar forms of innovative behaviour – we are actually not terribly convinced by the use of the term 'complex system' in the sense that it applies a specific label to a particular set of industries while at the same time excluding a range of other (presumably simple system) industries whose systemic properties are non-complex almost by definition. The problem appears to us to be one of conflating the notion of a complicated product with the wider concept of complex system, with all the associated characteristics and properties that were noted in Chapter 2. This then appears to allow the authors to contrast innovative behaviour in non-complex industries, for example, as that of the 'conventional technology race/market contest Schumpeterian model' where innovations are produced by R&D departments and then selected differentially by market forces. In fact, however, not all analysts would accept either the conventionality of that (neo-Darwinian) model nor its simplicity. For example, as we saw in Section 3.4 there are a whole range of authors who would certainly see themselves as operating within the Schumpeterian tradition, but who would not accept the nature of the 'conventional' model as described by Miller et al.

For many of these writers the important feature of much economic change is precisely that for long periods technological evolution can proceed in ways that are almost independent of economic production, mediated by institutional changes and often depending heavily on cooperative (Lamarckian?) behaviour on the part of the many stakeholders who have relevant interests and expertise. For example, in recent years significant sections of Japanese industry has been fostered by pre-competitive research catalysed by the Ministry of International Trade and Industry (MITI) but predominantly financed on a cooperative basis by firms who are actually competitors with one another (Fransman, 1995). In industries such as protein engineering and high superconductivity ceramics (by no means uncomplicated industries), such has been the 'complexity' of the science base that there is really no alternative to novel forms of cooperation if international competitiveness is to be established and maintained. Similar results are beginning to appear in industries reliant on the search for and classification of micro-organisms.[19] Nor is the phenomenon confined to the high-tech sectors. For example, Clark and Juma (1992) show how relatively unsophisticated technologies such as photovoltaics and fuel ethanol underwent complex evolutionary processes lasting for many decades before they began to emerge on to the economic arena.[20] Industries such as flight simulators are certainly concerned with complicated products but to apply the generic label of 'complex systems' to them can be highly misleading.

Another emergent tradition that has begun to capture wide interest is that of the identification of new models of industrial organisation which stress the systemic nature of much modern industrial production and by extension, as it were, the greater productivity of industrial systems that try to come to terms with this fact. In a recent paper Humphrey (1995) categorises important examples of this tradition as *flexible specialisation* (Piore and Sabel, 1984), *lean production* (Womack et al., 1990), *systemofacture* (Hoffman and Kaplinsky, 1988), *post Fordism* (Jessop et al., 1988) and *industrial districts* (Sengenberger and Pyke, 1991), and points out that many of the properties of such models may have important implications for development possibilities in the Third World.

While much of this emergent interest has focused on the apparent success of the South East Asian, Newly Industrialising Countries (NICs) as adopters of Japanese management styles and methods, what is also of particular interest are the experiences of small manufacturing establishments in parts of Southern Europe, firms that would not in any sense be labelled complex by the layperson but which collectively display properties that should certainly be described as systemic in the formal sense we have tried to define in Chapter 2. Very often, for example, such firms 'cluster' in relatively small geographical locations and are hence able to benefit each other synergistically through mobilising collective services, improving information access, permitting a greater degree of specialisation than would otherwise be feasible, acting as a means of substantial skill improvements, and generally improving the competitiveness of the region as a whole.

The systemic nature of such clusters may be seen, for example, in terms of the degree of *cooperative information flow* amongst constituent nodal firms who often engage in various forms of joint action designed to improve collective benefit. Sometimes these relations take the form of *nested hierarchies* where, for example, a parent firm acts as a prime contractor to a web of primary and secondary subcontractors who in some cases are virtually indistinguishable from cottage-scale family firms. Often such arrangements take the form of (Koestlerian) *associative nets* or *networks* with considerable social, economic and informational interchange taking place amongst the subcontracting firms as a necessary counterpart to productive activities of the system as a whole. Such systems are also *evolutionary*, enjoying economies of scale and scope as competitive pressures lead to innovative behaviour. Finally their systemic nature allows industrial clusters to demonstrate *resilience* since it often permits 'an additional degree of flexible response in unpredictable and turbulent environments'.[21]

In short the systemic nature of such clusters, while highly complex, by no means implies a correspondence with the types of sophisticated industrial products described by Miller et al. Both are systemic. Indeed both are complex, although one can argue a point about the *degree* of complexity.[22] But whatever may be the distinguishing features of the latter group it is incorrect to summarise these under the label of 'complex systems'. We are nearer the mark when we return to the process of economic differentiation outlined towards the end of Chapter 2. There we saw how the division of labour and specialisation of function in the early industrialising countries led progressively to the complex deepening of production systems and ultimately to what has come to be defined as the 'fordist' or 'mass production' paradigm of economic production under which a particular form of industrial organisation became clearly very efficient.

It has been one of the considerable achievements of the group of analysts summarised by Humphrey (1995) above, to show how the latter part of the twentieth century has begun to witness the decline of this paradigm and its replacement with a qualitatively different form of industrial organisation, often given the labels Japanese management techniques (JMTs) or total quality management (TQM). The characteristics of this systemic type (emphasising, for example, just-in-time inventory procedures and cellular factory layout) have been extensively explored by Kaplinsky (1994), Schmitz (1989), Humphrey (1995), Bessant(1990), Womack et al. (1990) and many, many others. However it is not correct to suggest that this emergent paradigm is systemic whereas the old one was not. On the contrary the mass production paradigm, as a particular form of economic organisation, was highly systemic in virtually all the definitional respects we have outlined. The point is that as the twentieth century has progressed the mass production paradigm, as a form of industrial organisation, has increasingly become an *inefficient* system. Firms that stick to it are being outcompeted by those who are searching for new sources of organisational competitiveness. But it is not the fact that these newer forms are systemic that is making the difference. It is rather that *systemic changes* are part of the evolutionary dynamic. In many respects production based on JMT systems is simply more efficient than that based on mass production systems.

3.6 MODELLING EVOLUTIONARY CHANGE

Economic evolution, therefore, occurs as a result of the competitive process, mediated by cooperative arrangements, in general – and in particular as a result of investments in technical change (broadly defined) and how these investments relate to the wider technological system, which itself is continuously evolving. The final question to raise in this chapter is actually the most difficult since it requires us to focus what is clearly an extremely complex process into a set of tools of use to a development planner and policy maker. The question is, how do we model economic change in ways that allow the policy maker scope to intervene?

As we noted in Chapter 1, the traditional means has been that of macro modelling, that is, modelling the whole economic system in terms of the interrelations among macroeconomic aggregates. In this approach technological change (the primary 'causal agent') is 'exogenous' and, with a few exceptions, microeconomic behaviour is also excluded. And yet if we begin to include the complex microeconomic behaviour outlined in the previous section above, the model would very quickly become difficult to handle. Not only would it be enormously time-consuming to specify the necessary equations, but also there would arise significant data problems when attempting to calibrate them.

Fortunately, however, it is possible to provide a dynamic account of economic evolution using another approach – that of spatial modelling – which incidentally, has the advantage that it directly includes the behaviour of the household sector as an integral part of the model. The technique used is to start from the simple circular flow model outlined at the beginning of this chapter, but to split the economic system into a number of regions between which flow people and resources. The households in each region are viewed as migrating from region to region to take advantage of (perceived) better economic opportunities and other benefits, while the productive sector in each region (which actually helps to give rise to these differential opportunities) fluctuates in size depending upon the investment activities of its constituent firms.

We shall describe this model and how it may be used in the ensuing chapters but it is important for the reader to understand why this form of modelling is being adopted. The first reason, which we have already mentioned, is the complexity of relations in the productive sector which render the specification of competitive firm behaviour almost impossible. A second reason is that spatial models explicitly include also household behaviour, whereas concentrating on the productive sector exclusively requires that we ignore households. A third advantage (which we shall emphasise later) is that our spatial model allows us to start off from a simple level and then gradually take into account more complex relationships as data permit. Indeed (and this is a fourth point) spatial modelling techniques bring the analyst much closer to data than traditional economic models where, as we argued in Chapter 1, there is no real sense in which models are allowed to change to reflect new empirical evidence. Finally, our approach specifically allows for the wider environment to be integrated into the planning process.

However, there is a more fundamental rationale for the suggested break with macroeconomic planning, and that relates to the *time horizons relevant to the analysis of economic evolution.* For viewing economic development as a process of structural change requires of necessity that we investigate the *strategic*, as opposed to the *immediate*, behaviour of the actors involved. Much of standard macroeconomic analysis has been designed as an aid to the short-term management of economic systems, particularly with respect to difficult issues of national income stabilisation (inflation, unemployment and the like) which continue to occupy the professional lives of many decision makers. In a sense we are bypassing these controversies and hence moving the whole agenda on to a longer-term perspective, a necessary condition we would argue, for the proper analysis of development issues. It follows that the emphasis upon the decision to migrate (for households) and the decision to invest (for firms) has been placed there precisely because these are the important strategic decisions. What we are concerned with is the provision of decision tools which will help the analysis of the long-term, structural development of economic systems. This does not mean that short-term macroeconomic instability is unimportant. What it does mean, however, is that the tools to resolve them are not necessarily the same as those required for the monitoring and control of long-term development.

3.7 CONCLUSIONS

We began this chapter with the intention of exploring how feasible it is to define economic processes in systemic terms. The main reason for so doing is to provide a basis for the planning models to be discussed later in this book, but very much in our minds also has been our critique of conventional development planning models set out in Chapter 1. Our principle conclusion is that it is the neo-Schumpeterian literature in economics which has been making the most important contribution to our understanding of how economic systems evolve. That is to say, the evolutionary drive behaviour outlined in Chapter 2 is most clearly mirrored in the neo-Schumpeterian approach.

What this approach does is to emphasise the importance of novelty in the economic process which in turn stresses the role of technological change. It turns out, however, that economic evolution is an extremely complicated process (which is one reason, possibly, why conventional economic planning models have taken the forms they have) and one that does not lend itself easily to modelling activity. This is particularly the case if the approach focuses directly on the productive sector and hence on interfirm competitive rivalry. However, as we shall go on to point out in subsequent chapters, the use of spatial models can provide decision tools which, though not capable of capturing the full details of the economic process, enable us to explore planning possibilities in ways which hold out considerable promise for the future. They can also do three more things. Firstly they can begin to help us to think more clearly about the actual *structure* of an economic system and how this changes over time. Secondly they can help us to integrate the *co-evolutionary* behaviour of natural systems. Finally, as we shall go on to point out, the models can be used as *decision tools* by those directly involved in system intervention and in a sense, therefore, permit emancipation from the 'expertise' embodied in more traditional modelling approaches.

One final point should perhaps be emphasised at this stage of our argument which runs as follows. Our overall objective is one of achieving greater understanding of the inner dynamics of economic systems as they unfold over time. In order to do this we have argued that it seems reasonable to view such systems as complex and evolutionary in character. It turns out, however, that the systems analogy has two dimensions – a cognitive one and a spatial one. Both are necessary elements of the temporal dynamics of economic systems. Ultimately our ability to influence this process will depend on our capacity to integrate both in our models.

NOTES

1   Examples of these and other authors may be found in Dosi et al. (eds) (1988).
2   See, for example, Clark and Juma (1992), Chapter 2.
3   It is true that microeconomic analysis formally extends into the long run – i.e. where the capital stock is allowed to vary – but this does not figure strongly in microeconomic texts.
4   See Fagerberg (1995) for an illustrative account of modern growth economics and related issues.
5   See Pereira-Mendes (1991), pp. 1–2.
6   For a short discussion of these and associated references see Clark (1985), Chapter 6.
7   See Soete (1986), p. 216.
8   See Clark and Juma (1992), Chapter 2.
9   See Koestler (1982), p. 463.
10 An important advantage in setting things out this way lies in the relative emphasis it gives to the heterogeneous forms of resource organisation that are feasible, as contrasted with standard economic theory where the undifferentiated 'firm' is the standard unit of resource.
11 There are many examples of such organisations, like those of the Protein Engineering Research Institution (PERI) and the International Superconductivity Research Centre (Istec) in Japan each of which is funded both by the industry itself and by the appropriate government body – in this case the Ministry of International Trade and Industry (MITI).
12 For a discussion of this and related issues see Altshuler et al. (eds) (1984), and Hobday (1994a). An updated account of the Altshuler et al. book, which deals with the advent of lean production in the globalised automobile industry may be found in Womak et al. (1990). See also Graves (1991). A more general account dealing with the Japanese 'Kaizen' in many industrial contexts may be found in Imai (1986).
13 The original source for this discussion is Schumpeter (1934), but a more recent comprehensive source is Dosi et al. (1988). For a detailed discussion of the cognitive roots of economic systems, see Clark and Juma (1992).
14 One of the authors has discussed these aspects in some detail in Clark and Juma (1992).
15 See Clark and Juma (1992) for a discussion of the entropic nature of technological flows. For a recent account of how some modern Japanese firms are encouraging their research scientists to publish results, and thereby 'trade' knowledge, see Hicks (1995).
16 See Constant (1973, 1980) and for a more detailed discussion, Clark (1987).
17 See, for example, Gardiner and Rothwell (1985).
18 See Miller et al. (1995), p. 1.
19 See Pollak (1995).
20 There are many other examples of this genre. See, for example, Rosenberg (1976), Constant (1973).
21 See Humphrey (1995), p. 2.
22 As far as we know neither Miller et al. (1995), nor anyone else has proposed a widely accepted measure of the degree of complexity.

4. Spatial Modelling[1]

4.1 INTRODUCTION

As we have outlined earlier in the text a major issue in contemporary development planning concerns how to ensure sustainability in economic systems whilst at the same time ensuring rising living standards for their inhabitants. An important part of the problem lies in the evolutionary complexity of such systems whereby the interactive behaviour of relevant actors is very difficult to predict with any realism. A related difficulty concerns how one defines the system under investigation. Traditionally analysts (who are often economists) tend to define quite tightly in order to reach robust solutions to problems, but they do so at the cost of leaving out behaviour which cannot easily be encompassed within their models (i.e. in formal terms rendering such behaviour exogenous). This often means that vital interrelationships are ignored whose impact can make a considerable difference to people's livelihoods.

Following our discussion of economic systems in Chapter 3, our purpose in this chapter is to suggest a class of simulation techniques which specifically take into account systemic complexity and which may be used (alongside more conventional techniques) to explore the complex evolutionary behaviour of economic systems in ways which may help deal with these sorts of problems. Because there are important methodological issues involved, Section 4.2 provides a stylised summary of conventional approaches to economic planning, stressing that although such models have an important role to play, their use at a strategic level has important drawbacks. Section 4.3 outlines a model of the Senegal economy (described in detail in Appendix I) as a specific example of what we have in mind, while Section 4.4 contrasts the strengths and weaknesses of this rather new approach. In Chapter 5 we go on to extend the approach to include the integrated analysis of the natural system but we should stress that our main aim at this stage is suggestive. More detailed research will be required before our methodology can be seen to be fully established.

4.2   PLANNING AND SYSTEMIC KNOWLEDGE

All acts of development planning presume some understanding of the economic system which is being 'acted upon'. By this we mean that operational goals or targets can be achieved only if the means (or policy interventions) are well conceived in terms of how the system in question actually works. Conventionally, development planning is conducted at three levels of decreasing aggregation – the whole economy, the sector, the project.[2] The first of these is conceived of as an economic system of resources (inputs) and commodities (outputs) where flows of resources per unit of time are converted by a productive system into flows of commodities, and where the common dimension of all flows is monetary.

Resources may be categorised into different conventional categories (e.g. natural resources, labour and capital) and the relationship may be described mathematically in functional terms:

$$Q = Q(R, L, K) \qquad\qquad (4.1)$$

where Q = output vector,
             R = natural resources vector,
             L = abour vector,
             K = capital vector.

Conventional economic theory makes the further assumption that this 'macro' system is a closed one where the owners of the resources (the households) are also the same economic agents who consume the commodities after they have been produced. Graphically these relationships may be portrayed in terms of the well-known circular flow of income diagram, introduced in Chapter 3 (and repeated here, as Figure 4.1), which is often then modified to include specific categories of 'systemic openness', namely, foreign trade, government activity, and disturbance arising out of the behaviour of savers and investors.

Development planning concerns usually the increase of the capacity of the production sector to produce goods and services, and hence relates to the 'K' resource in equation (4.1) and the 'S/I' instability focus in equation (4.2). This is not necessarily required of course since a) economic systems can become more productive through augmenting natural resources or the skill levels of the labour force and b) most economic change requires synchronous shifts of all three resource types. But as an operational variable I has a range of distinct advantages (e.g. it can be more easily targeted and valued than the others). The real problem is, however, that the analysis as outlined provides no theory of change – no account of precisely how the productive capacity of P gets augmented over time. Instead, growth of the production system is assumed to be a simple linear function of investment, with the long-term 'behaviour' of the macrosystem from a planning perspective reduced to a (Harrod/Domar) relationship of the following general form:

$$g = s/v \qquad (4.2)$$

where $g = dQ/dt$,
$\quad s = S/Y$,
$\quad v = I/Q$,
$\quad Q = Y$,

g will be higher the greater is the average propensity of households to save (s) and the smaller is the capital/output ratio (v).

Figure 4.1 The circular flow of income in the macroeconomy

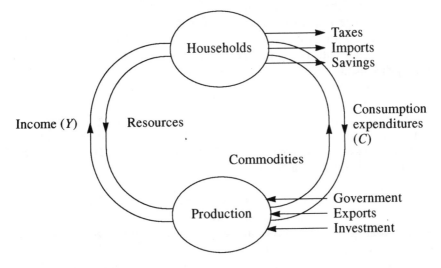

4.2.1 Sectoral and Project Planning

Thus the problem with 'macro' analysis is really that it provides a very crude representation of how the system works and hence gives little indication of how to intervene effectively.[3] For this reason equation (4.2) usually provides only a broad framework or target, while the economic system is then conceptually broken down into more manageable microstates. The first of these portrays the actual structure of the macrosystem in terms of sectoral interrelationships, taking the form of intersectoral resource flows described by an input–output table. Sectoral categories (e.g. agriculture, industry, services, communications, etc. – further divided into smaller categories) are chosen on conventional grounds and on the basis of adequate data. The input–output table is then established and provides a structural account of the economic system in question, which then permits the planner to explore the consequences of intervention at the sectoral levels once the consequences of intervention have worked through the system.[4]

Naturally the validity of these predictions depends upon how good a representation of the economic system this is. An input–output table may be characterised by a series of linear equations whose parameters reflect technological conditions appertaining at the time the relevant data were collected. Clearly therefore there will be problems associated with structural change which will become greater the longer is the planning time horizon. There are also problems associated with the quality of the data themselves and with their coverage. One very important example here is the environmental costs of economic activity which are not normally enumerated (partly it is true because of lack of adequate information) but which could in principle give a totally different picture of the resource consequences of economic development. Nevertheless, the great advantage of the input–output table is that it provides, as it were, a photograph of the economic system over a particular (short) time segment and the act of constructing it provides additional detailed understanding to the economic planner.

From the standpoint of its use as a planning tool, perhaps its major drawback is that it cannot tell the planner how to proceed at the 'micro' level – what specific projects to invest in, how to intervene to raise the rate of private sector investment in specific cases and so on. For this reason economic planners use techniques like that of social cost/benefit analysis (SCBA) to rank competing projects within sectors and to assess the viability of particular projects which have been proposed to multilateral funding agencies (like the World Bank, the regional development banks, or the EC). At a more general level they use the tax system, procurement policy, regulatory policy, technology policy and other devices to influence economic behaviour in ways seen to be consistent with overall planning goals. In this manner the economic 'microstates' are shifted in 'desirable' directions, in ways they would not have shifted in the absence of such intervention.

At each level of aggregation, then, the economic planner has internalised some model about how the economic system 'works', i.e. how resources are transformed into commodities at micro level, how the price system combined with state regulation allocates these commodities amongst alternative economic uses, how at any point of time the planner may summarise 'knowledge' about the outcomes of this process through conventional techniques of social accounting which describe the economic system's 'structure', and how the productive potential of the whole system is reflected in some measure of overall economic performance. It is this 'knowledge' which allows him to justify acts of policy intervention which will in some sense 'make the system work better'.

4.2.2 Diagnosis

What then are the problems inherent in this broad planning approach? To us these are that insufficient attention is paid to systemic complexity – to interdependencies amongst the component economic agents of the system in question, to the processes through which substructures co-evolve to produce macro outcomes, and to the problem of (lack of) a complete capacity on the part of the planner to obtain and process relevant information. Of course most sophisticated planners are well aware that their conventional tools are very imperfect and that for many reasons their predictions are bound to be wrong. Nevertheless, they argue that unless we are to leave decisions of resource allocation completely to the free market (and practically no one takes this extreme position), then it is better to base policy intervention on the tools that we have than not to do so, if only because the alternative of power politics would lead to worse outcomes. In any case sensible use of such tools, combined with regular monitoring and evaluation procedures, should mitigate in practice many of the more obvious defects. While we have some sympathy with this broad position, we feel nevertheless that as the twentieth century draws to a close it is distinctly second best. And the main reason for arguing this is very simply that in a world which is evolving very fast, it is becoming increasingly artificial (and indeed misleading) to act as if economic systems can be regarded as closed and linear, with identifiable, homogeneous and measurable inputs yielding corresponding outputs using technological processes which do not change and where extra-systemic effects can be conveniently ignored (or treated as exogenous).

In what follows we suggest an alternative approach using a specific example of resource management analysis through which the system under investigation is specified in behavioural terms as a set of interactive subsystems which may then be fitted to historic data and used to develop risk scenarios for the future. The advantage of this approach is that it may be used as an interactive tool on the part of policy makers, improving their understanding of the system in question and (hopefully) leading to better interventions. Nor should its use preclude conventional approaches, since we shall try to show that it can provide broad scenarios within which more conventional techniques may be used. In this way the policy-making process can be enriched to the ultimate benefit of the system under consideration.

Figure 4.2   Strategic behaviour of households and firms

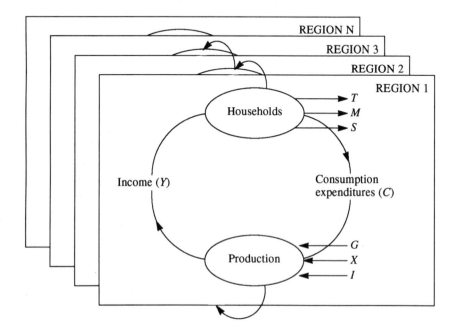

As outlined briefly at the end of the previous chapter, the approach is based upon an account of the strategic behaviour of households and firms in any economic system, that is, their decision making with respect to the long term as contrasted with that of the short term. A good way of describing this is to return to the macroeconomic diagram outlined above as Figure 4.1 which portrays the latter as circular resource flows, the households selling resources to the firms, who then 'add value' before selling them back to the households in the form of commodities. Figure 4.2 then portrays the complementary long-term behaviour as migratory behaviour, on the part of households, and investment behaviour, on the part of firms – in each case across regions or zones into which the system has been divided. Such behaviour is clearly strategic in nature since it is only normally undertaken with a view to payoffs expected to accrue over many years, and may thus be distinguished from the shorter-term 'maximising' behaviour of conventional economic analysis. It is perhaps easiest to describe it in detail within the context of a specific case, that of the Senegal model.

4.3   THE SENEGAL MODEL

The Senegal model has been developed as a decision tool for policy makers in Senegal. It consists of sets of interacting equations each of which represents the change in some characteristic variable occurring at a particular time and place. This could be, for example, the change taking place in a zone (or region), of the resident population, in an economic or subsistence activity, in the amount and quality of the soil there, or in the water availability at the location.[5] These changes occur because of the existence of processes, events and mechanisms operating at the different locations within the system. For example, population change in any region occurs because of births, deaths, and in-and-out migration, and similarly water which is used there flows into and out of the region, and may also be produced there by wells and springs. Each of these terms reflects the rate of occurrence of different processes and individual events, of which there may be different types, and this rate of occurrence may itself be influenced both by the values of internal variables (e.g. the size of the population, the area of some crop) and parameters (e.g. soil fertility, the fecundity of the local population), as well as by exogenous parameters such as rainfall, river flow and migration.

Each equation in the model is made up of terms representing the effects of such mechanisms and processes. Most of the equations fall into two main groups corresponding to the types of actors whose behaviour is fundamental to spatial evolution: (i) the households whose migratory behaviour determines population movements, and (ii) the producers whose behaviour determines the nature and extent of economic activity in each region and the flow of resources between regions. When fully developed the model will also include a third group of equations which concern changes in ecological populations – e.g. of water availability, of soil and minerals, and of noxious deposits – although readers will be able to see in Chapter 5 a very simple water model that has been included as part of the scenario development for the island of Crete.

The way the model works is that the behaviour of any one set of actors in any one region is continually changing as a result of first, the behaviour of all the other actors (in all regions) and second, the information channels which determine how such behaviour is perceived. For example, Figure 4.3, which describes the local population dynamics in a region, illustrates the positive feedbacks that have been represented mathematically in the model to capture the mechanisms by which populations behave and migrate. Cultural preferences are explicitly modelled in terms of the way in which the population in a region values the perceived costs and rewards or social status in their community. These perceptions, depicted as a cloud of rewards and costs, determine in the model how the population in any region reacts to current economic and social conditions. The model is calibrated using past data until it regenerates the temporal evolution of the system up to the present time on the basis of the fundamental processes which underlie that system.   It may then be used to assess the consequences of future scenarios and thence to guide policy making in a more desirable direction than would have been the case without the use of the model. For example an earlier version of the model generated changes that occurred between 1979 and 1988 in regional populations, economic activities and certain natural resources (Figure 4.4).

Figure 4.3   Local population dynamics in a region

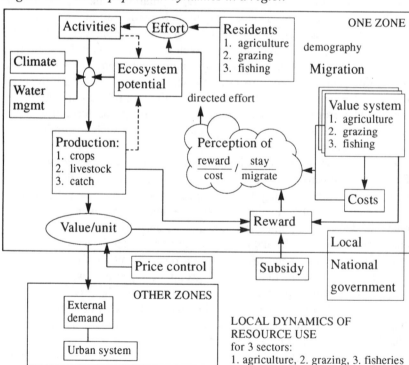

Figure 4.4   Population dynamics in Senegal

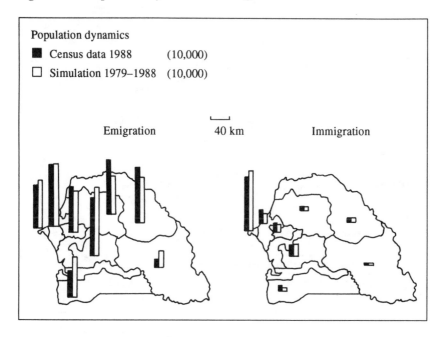

Population dynamics
■ Census data 1988   (10,000)
☐ Simulation 1979–1988   (10,000)

Emigration   40 km   Immigration

Again for purposes of exposition it is useful to explore a variant of Figure 4.1 where we outlined the simple circular flow of income diagram which underlies so much of conventional economic modelling. First of all we split the economic system into a number of regions or zones. Figure 4.5 then depicts the evolutionary behaviour for any economic sector in any region in terms of the interactive behaviour of households and firms. For example, as firms expand (as the result of an increase in demand for their product) they increase the demand for labour in the zone, wages rise and vacancies are created. This encourages migration from other zones which in turn has two effects. First it tends to reduce wage costs, thereby increasing profits. Second, it increases the local markets for the products of this sector and hence encourages further investment. Of course such a positive feedback loop is not without its own potential constraints. For example, scarce resources at the margin (such as land or water) may push up costs. Or improved productivity in other zones may reduce the competitiveness of local firms. If that happened to a marked extent, the sector would decline in the region leading perhaps to net emigration, and so on.

Figure 4.5   Evolutionary behaviour in a region

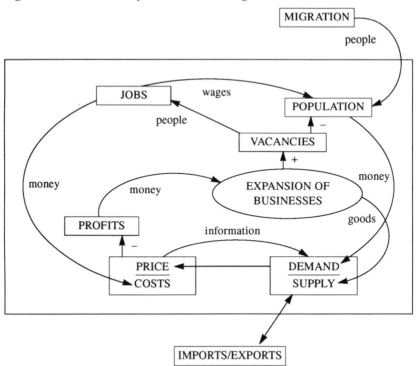

A detailed description of a current version of the simulation model is provided in Appendix I, but a simplified outline omitting the investment function may be described as follows. We suppose that the economic system is split into *n* regions (1, 2, 3, ...*i*, *j*, ...*n*) and *m* sectors (1, 2, 3, ...*l*, ...*m*) and consider economic activities at the level of these sectors and regions. For every sector and every region there is a similar set of variables in it. Strategic investment behaviour in each sector/region then proceeds as a function of relative 'attractivities' which depend upon changes in relative profit rates and land scarcities. These in turn are found by comparing demand and supply conditions in the relevant sector/region which themselves depend upon price, cost and income conditions. Finally aggregate behaviour at key temporal stages is computed by summing over each region and sector. The second type of strategic behaviour, population migration of households, is calculated in a similar manner, that is, by decisions being determined by a sequence of relative attractivities which in turn depend upon labour market conditions across regions and sectors aggregated at various stages in the calculation.

For purposes of illustration a simplified example of how the procedure works may be seen by considering any sector L and any geographic region j, and asking the question: what factors will influence the final consumption behaviour of consumers in j with respect to purchases of L from all other regions $i = 1,2,3, ...i, ..., n$? In order to answer this question we may define a region's relative 'attractivity' in the following way. Define the consumption attractivity of commodities purchased from region i, from the standpoint of consumers in region j as

$$^{L}Catt_{ij} = e^{-R}\left(^{L}P_{i} + TC_{ij}\right) \tag{4.3}$$

where R =   represents a response rationality parameter.
           $^{L}P_{i}$ =   price of L in region i.
           TC_{ij} =   transport costs for a unit of L between i and j.

In order to find the relative attractivity of region i, viewed from region j, we must now sum over all the potential sources of L from j:

$$^{L}Catt_{j} = \sum_{i} {}^{L}Catt_{ij} + e^{-R}\left(^{WL}P + TC_{jw}\right) \tag{4.4}$$

where ^{WL}P =   world price
           TC_{jw} =   transport costs from j to the world market.

The relative attractivity of i viewed from j is therefore:

$$\frac{^{L}Catt_{j}}{^{L}Catt_{ij}} = {}^{L}RCatt_{ij} \tag{4.5}$$

The fraction of demand situated at j that is likely to be satisfied by a supply from i is $^{L}RCatt_{ij}$. If β_{L} is the fraction of total income that is directed to sector L then, from points within the system,

Final Demand on L falling on $i = \sum_{j} \beta_{L} Y \times {}^{L}RCatt_{ij}$ (4.6)

A similar calculation may be carried out to estimate intersectorial demand, which in this case we shall assume also contains investment demand, and we are now in a position to compute the total overall demand falling on any zone i. This is equal to disposable income partitioned by a set of sectorial parameters β_{L} + intersectorial demands + external demand from the rest of the world (exports). Disposable income is made up of wages + rents received.

$$^{L}D_i = \sum_j \left(\beta_L \times Y_j * {}^{L}D_j \right) - {}^{L}RCatt_{ij} + \frac{^{XL}De^{-R}\left({}^{L}P_i + {}^{L}TC_{iw} \right)}{^{L}Catt_i} \tag{4.7}$$

where ^{XL}D =   external demand for L
            $^{L}D_j$ =   demand for L in region j

We are finally therefore in a position to compare total demand falling on i (in sector L) with supply of L in i. This is given by:

$$^{L}S_i = {}^{L}E_i \times {}^{L}P_i \times {}^{L}Pr\, y_i \tag{4.8}$$

where E =   employment,
           Pry =   productivity of labour.

It is then relatively simple to model the change in economic activity which will result from any disequilibrium between supply and demand in terms of a rate of desired expansion. For example, in an earlier version of the model, expansion was defined simply in terms of equation (4.9), namely:

$$\frac{\partial Q_i^l}{\partial t} = \eta^l \times P_i^l \left(\frac{D_i^l}{S_i^l} - 1 \right) \tag{4.9}$$

However, in later versions we have used a rate of change of jobs function described by equations (AI.19), (AI.20) and (AI.21) in Appendix I. As profits increase in any sector/region so too will investment, which in turn will create vacancies. The rate of change in jobs is then described as a set of functions relating vacancies, investment rates and past labour market conditions. The advantage of this formulation is that it explicitly includes investment behaviour as part of the overall model, thus improving its realism.

     It is important finally to be clear about how this very simple model works. Its starting point is one of proposing that the economic behaviour of *individual* actors (say, consumption behaviour of households) in each region is influenced strongly by perceptions regarding the spatial origin of commodities. In this way microeconomic behaviour is directly built into the model as is the spatial dimension. The *micro/macro interface* is then achieved by a summation technique in which macro behaviour is estimated by summing behaviour over households and regions in such a way that it is always possible to isolate the impact of economic demand (in this case consumption demand) on any one region. In a sense then, what drives the model is a calculation of demand in relation to supply *in that region for the class of commodity under consideration.* Where demand is greater than supply during that time segment, output in the next time segment expands as a result of investment activity on the part of firms. Conversely where supply is greater than demand, investment, and therefore output, falls over time.

The resultant differential rate of change of economic activity across regions affects the migratory behaviour of households in a corresponding manner. Regions that are expanding tend on the whole to become richer and to offer greater employment opportunities, hence pulling in population from other regions. Conversely regions that are declining face long-term depopulation. And in turn such differential demographic behaviour affects investment activity in the ensuing periods, and so on in a sequence of endless evolutionary, and therefore *structural*, change. But it is important to recognise that the model is very simple indeed. There are only a small number of sectors and regions, and the equations and parameters are chosen to make calibration as easy as possible. The main aim is to ensure that the model provides as accurate an empirical description as possible of the evolutionary behaviour of the economic system under consideration (in this case Senegal), such that analysts and policy makers have a realistic starting point for scenario developments for the future.

Of course, as we go on to point out below, once an initial simple model has been built it is then a much more straightforward job to use such a model as a template for more sophisticated descriptions. Indeed model building and model use then themselves become an evolutionary process. For example, we shall see in Chapter 5 that using the model in practical ways, as a decision tool, enables analysts to see much more clearly its weaknesses, hence pointing the way for further data collection, model revision, and so on. The point is that the overall model-building activity represents an exercise in simulating the *strategic behaviour* of an economic system, an exercise which therefore abstracts from short-term socio-economic factors and hence can more easily be used to help long-term planning.

4.3.1 Natural Resources and Perceptions

Thus far we have not included natural resources (or more important, the environment) in our exposition, but of course the evolution of the natural system in each region is of central importance[6] and there will eventually be a complete set of dynamical equations for this element. In fact a more general diagram of the Senegal model would look more like Figure 4.6 where strategic change is seen in terms of the long-term behaviour of three subsystems.

The natural resource system provides resources for use by households and firms which if not replaced will lead to environmental degradation. At the same time the interactive dynamics which we have represented mathematically in the model capture the ways in which households and firms interact spatially. Notice again that Figure 4.6 is quite distinct from Figure 4.1, the basic economic diagram, which depicts circular flows of money and goods moving between households and firms.   Figure 4.1 concerns essentially the *short-term* functioning only of the economic system at a point in time.   In contrast, Figure 4.6 includes natural resources as an integral feature of the economic system and focuses on the entirely different issue of *long-term* change.

Figure 4.6   The inclusion of the natural system

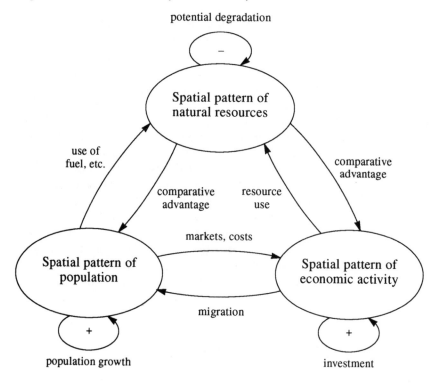

Here perception (influenced also by cultural factors) plays an important role. Thus from the standpoint of populations, perceptions of rewards and costs determine how the population in any given zone reacts to the current economic and social conditions. If the existing conditions in another region *j*, or regions, are perceived as more 'attractive' then a certain number of the population will emigrate from *i* to *j*, although since we are dealing with a *distribution* of perceptions there will always be a (small) proportion of people who see things the other way around and hence migrate from *j* to *i*.

Figure 4.7   Example of food aid

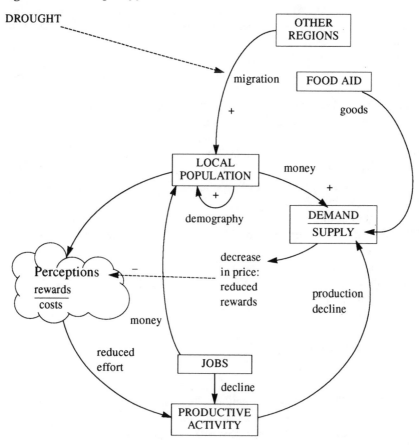

These perceptions of rewards and costs also direct the choice of productive activity, and hence the local 'culture' of the population in a region. The infrastructure and available resources (land, water, irrigation, nutrients in the soil) then determine the actual productivity of the efforts invested in the chosen activities, and the yields obtained in the region over time. This production will generate some given level of rewards and costs to the population engaged in that activity, depending on *their* values. Differences between these perceived rewards and costs lead to a new pattern of investment in activities, reflecting higher expected rewards and cultural diversity of the population. Hence we see that as the different groups of the population in each region act according to different perceptions, they then create a new reality which turns out to be unlike what any of them had previously perceived. These new conditions then modify people's perceptions, which generate new mental maps, actions, and so forth.

It is important to note that such disjunctions between perception and reality are not only very common in development planning, they can also lead to counter-intuitive behaviour. A well-known example of this is the case of food aid where, as many authorities have pointed out,[7] the advent of food aid often actually leads to changes that set back development in the system as a whole. In fact our model demonstrates the kinds of mechanisms which could generate such counter-intuitive results, for example in Figure 4.7 where food aid depresses prices, reduces perceptions of relative economic rewards on the part of producers who in turn reduce output, thus increasing the need for food aid.

At the same time availability of cheap food encourages migration from other regions to where the food aid arrives (usually at the capital city or a major port) thereby creating even more problems. This example demonstrates the potential of this modelling tool to examine the possible effects of interventions or development schemes to assist decision makers in their very difficult task.

4.4 EVALUATION

A number of distinctive features of this general approach should now be stressed. Firstly, our model is neither closed nor deterministic. This is so because new information is continually reaching the actors altering their subsequent behaviour in ways that can be anticipated but which will inevitably prove to be inaccurate as time unfolds. Secondly the system behaves as a resultant of the behaviour of two subsystems, the households and the firms' each of whose behaviour depends upon the independent behaviour of the other. Thus the decision of firms to invest (and therefore locate) more in any area will alter the conditions (and therefore the determinants) of subsequent household behaviour. This in turn, however, will alter firm behaviour leading to new location decisions and so on. Thirdly behaviour is heuristic in the sense that the parameters assigned to the model's equations are not to be seen as accurate representations of a permanent set of relationships, but rather as the sum of temporary views of the actors themselves with respect to how they ought to behave *at that time*, given their own intentionality, the relative attractivity of locations and other relevant information. Although calibration gives the appearance of determinism, in reality the model is only a broad analytical tool which can be used in a number of ways by the analyst.

However, by far the most important feature of our approach is that it is really an interactive methodology rather than a model. Indeed we take the view that since economic systems are continuously evolving there is little point in trying to represent their long-term behaviour by mechanical models which are certain to be out of date even before they have been built. In order to illustrate the interactive properties of our methodology let us suppose a specific (hypothetical) problem facing the Senegalese government, namely, that of economic decline in regions remote from the main centres of activity, particularly the capital Dakar. Clearly there will be a variety of policy responses which the government could make which in general would depend upon specific circumstances in each region. Let us suppose, however, that it is decided to boost agricultural production and incomes by policies designed to increase planting of specific crops in each region. Using our model it would then be possible to explore the regional consequences. For example, the decision to convert 4,000 Ha in region *i* to rice production could be projected into its resultant effects on the economic system as a whole in addition to its effects on that region.

Of particular importance here is the strategy's ecological sustainability. Massive alienation of land to paddy production would of course have enormous socio-economic implications in the short-to-medium term, but sustainability would also depend crucially on impacts on water, soils, nutrients and accretions of noxious deposits. By running the model using a range of assumptions affecting these (and other) variables, it is possible to calculate the probability that the region in question will become unsustainable over a given period and therefore whether the policy on rice production is a sustainable one. If it is not (or at least if the accompanying risks are judged too high), then a more conservative set of plans may be adopted and evaluated as before.[8]

What it is important to realise is that planning of this type is both heuristic and interactive – heuristic in the sense of narrowing down strategic options in advance of more concrete project selection, interactive in so far as the model represents a decision tool for use by policy makers themselves in conjunction with clients. Clients (e.g. local farmers' organisations) may be consulted about the local realism of the model's consumptions which can be changed very easily. Policy makers themselves can use the model as an aid to their own deliberations and discussions. Indeed the interactive nature of the model means that learning can take place, so that the model may be refined progressively as new knowledge is obtained. To begin with (and during the initial calibration phase) it tends to be fairly crude and simple, mainly because of data and computational constraints. However, initial use of the model suggests how the pursuit of relevant empirical research should then take place – i.e. to generate new and better data – while enriching the model's complexity gradually improves its realism over time. Finally, unlike many recent attempts to model environmental impact, which treat this as an exogenous 'cost' of economic change,[9] our model has the capacity to endogenise environmental influences, as we shall see in the next chapter. Thus changes in water resources, for example, logically feed back into the economic behaviour of farmers, changing rates of economic growth and subsequent migratory patterns.

4.5   SOME CONCLUDING REMARKS

In this chapter we have begun to focus much more directly on the long term. By concentrating on the strategic aspects of planning horizons and by building interactive causal dynamics directly into our model, we would argue that we have gone beyond the conventional approach which presupposes fixed internal structures. Since the dynamic processes are also spatial and ecological, this means that the approach is no longer simply economic but is, in a fundamental sense, interdisciplinary. We are under no illusions about the inherent difficulties involved in modelling such complex open systems but would argue nevertheless that the reality of modern development requires a new approach. Such an approach is complementary to conventional approaches which work well over shorter time horizons where system parameters are relatively stable. What it does is to provide a set of decision tools which allow policy makers to take a longer view, and in so doing to build environmental sustainability directly into the planning process. The following chapter develops this theme in greater depth.

NOTES

1   This chapter is a revised version of a paper originally published in *Review of Political Economy*, **4** (3), 1992.
2   For a general discussion on the 'simple systems' logic of macroeconomic analysis, see Clark (1985), Chapter 3.
3   In practice many industrialised countries often develop medium-term plans of the type discussed in Chapter 1, above. Such plans include additional variables (e.g. the rate of interest and the money supply), and are used to make 'forecasts' of key policy variables such as the average price level or the public sector borrowing requirement.
4   For a general account of how the input–output table can be used as a planning tool, see Clark (1985), Chapter 3.
5   For a detailed discussion of this type of modelling procedure, see for example, Allen and Sanglier (1979, 1981). The Senegal model itself is described in some detail in IERC (1991).

6   For a more detailed discussion of the evolutionary dynamics of natural systems and modelling applications, see Perez-Trejo (1989).

7   See, for example, Clay (1981) and Morrison (1984).

8   We shall discuss the use of risk analysis to explore such policy options in Chapter 5, below.

9   See, for example, Pearce et al. (1989, Chapter 4).

5. The Model as a Decision Tool (A Crete Case Study)

5.1 INTRODUCTION

In the previous chapter we explored the general properties of an evolutionary economic system by means of a case study of Senegal. This chapter shows how such a model (in this case somewhat simplified) may be used as a decision tool by means of another regional case study – this time of the island of Crete in the Mediterranean. The chapter also provides rather more explicit details about how in principle the evolution of the natural system can be integrated with that of the socio-economic system, so as to provide a research methodology that can capture long-term structural change in both. The following section provides the overall rationale behind the Crete model, which has been one of helping to deal with problems of desertification in the Mediterranean basin. Section 5.3 briefly outlines the model itself while Section 5.4 goes on to illustrate its potential use as a decision tool by means of a scenario exploration of the expansion of tourism in Crete up to the year 2000.

The chapter then goes on to explore further areas of investigation using a methodology based upon a combination of computer scenario runs and risk analysis, discussed in general in Section 5.5. Section 5.6 explores the overall consistency of current Government of Crete policy towards tourist employment. Using randomly generated values for external potential demand for tourism, we show how it is possible to estimate probable jobs targets both for the year 2001 and for the intervening years. We then return to consideration of the α parameter, a key model parameter, in order to explore how changes in it are likely to result from actual job creation in tourism over a specified period. Section 5.7 examines how we might introduce the natural system into the analysis by introducing a very simple submodel of the groundwater system and run a risk scenario over a fifteen-year period from 1990 (i.e. to 2005). The objective here is to show how in principle it is relatively straightforward to integrate the natural and the economic systems in this type of policy analysis. Finally Section 5.8 makes some concluding points.

5.2   DESERTIFICATION IN THE MEDITERRANEAN BASIN

As we mentioned briefly in Chapter 1, not only do the environmental threats facing landscapes appear to be growing, but in addition the problems that managers and policy makers confront in dealing with them are magnified by the complexity of the many aspects that must be considered. In particular there are enormous difficulties in defining effective policy measures in the light of the evolutionary nature of underlying socio-economic and natural systems. Thus environmental problems are seldom localised. They usually affect large geographical areas involving complex interactions of land use and administrative jurisdiction, which often accounts for the failure of local and national authorities to develop effective policies for sustainable development. More specifically, land use patterns in the Mediterranean today are no longer an expression of the traditional values of local communities, but have been undergoing major transformations in recent decades driven largely by economic decisions of increasingly urbanised populations. These changes have had especially profound effects on certain landscapes of high vulnerability to erosion, land degradation and loss of biological potential (Blue Plan, 1992).

Figure 5.1 illustrates the ecological, economic and physical nature of the changes in the landscapes of the Mediterranean that have been occurring for the last 30 years, depicting the effects they have had on the different landscapes from the mountains, the terraced maquis, the low lands and the coastal zones. Today over 60% of the population lives in urban centres and the trend is expected to continue to increase (Coccossis, 1991). Even though there has been no major change in the proportion of land allocated to agriculture over the last 15 years, there has been a marked intensification of agricultural production which in turn has created an unprecedented risk of land degradation leading to soil erosion and marginalisation of many areas in the region. Thus mechanisation and irrigation have together increased by almost 50% between 1965 and 1982 (Coccossis, 1991). At the same time tourism has increased significantly during the period, attracting a significant proportion of the labour force from traditional jobs in rural agricultural regions to coastal cities driven by improved wages and the perceived attractiveness of urban living. Factors such as these have had a marked impact on the whole Mediterranean environment mainly due to land abandonment, which has affected traditional practices of terrace maintenance, increased the incidence of forest fires and hence further intensified the use of coastal zones.

Figure 5.1   Landscape changes in the Mediterranean

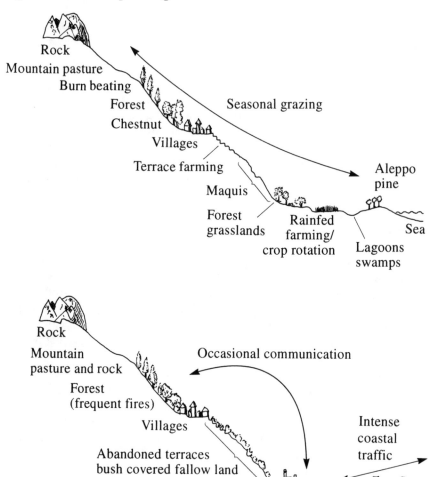

Figure 5.2   The ecosystem as a hierarchy of processes

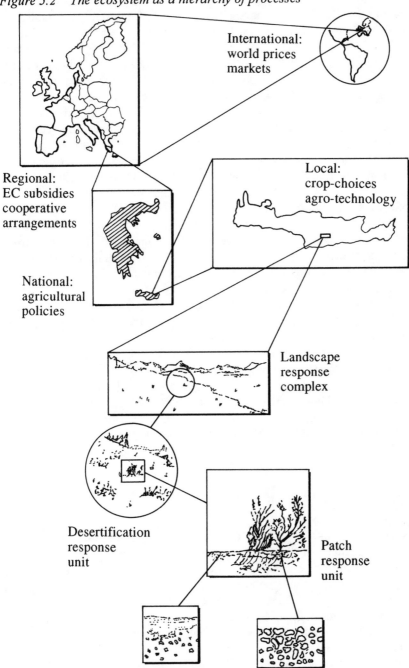

International:
world prices
markets

Regional:
EC subsidies
cooperative
arrangements

Local:
crop-choices
agro-technology

National:
agricultural
policies

Landscape
response
complex

Desertification
response
unit

Patch
response
unit

The Crete model was started under the auspices of the Medalus Project, a part of the EC EPOCH Programme of DG XII. Central to the overall aims of this project has been the view that the formulation of adequate policies to deal with desertification requires an approach that integrates the many disciplinary aspects that are of relevance to the complex biotic, abiotic, socio-economic and technological components of Mediterranean landscapes. As we mentioned in Chapter 1, such an approach may be contrasted with more traditional methods such as social cost/benefit analysis, environmental impact assessment and input–output models in assessing economic development scenarios.   Although useful, such methods do not directly account for the interdependence of processes underlying the biotic–abiotic–human dynamic, which in turn restricts their usefulness. The reasons for this are first, that the natural and physical processes (which collectively constitute what we perceive and describe as environmental) are in essence non-linear, second that the dynamics of socio-economic activity and its environmental effects have a spatial dimension which is a strong determinant of how these interactions actually unfold and of their ultimate effect on the environment, and third, that socio-economic and natural systems co-evolve and hence presumably require a co-evolutionary perspective for their analysis.   What was needed, therefore, was a methodology that focuses on a process-oriented research approach, where the overall system (socio-economic, ecological, environmental) is characterised in terms of processes at different temporal and spatial scales. In this way, a hierarchy of processes as illustrated in Figure 5.2, can provide a way of understanding what are the driving forces of land use changes in landscapes and how policy can act most effectively to mitigate the effects of land degradation and loss of biological potential that these changes might bring about. It was this thinking that led to the ongoing development of the Crete model.

5.3   THE CRETE MODEL

As with the Senegal model, the Crete model gives spatial dimensionality to the space available for any given economic activity, the choice of residence or migration of the population, and most importantly to the choices that the different sectors of the economy or consumers make in purchasing goods and services locally, from other regions, or from international markets; depending on location, price and choice of supplier. It consists of two sets of actors (or agents) – business firms which invest in different regions in response to economic signals, and households which migrate between regions, again largely for strategic socio-economic reasons. As each set of agents varies its behaviour it achieves impacts on regions which alter the behaviour of the other set in a continuous cycle of activity.

For example, the decision of households to migrate from region i to region j in response, say, to improved income-earning opportunities will alter relative economic conditions between the two regions which in turn will alter relative investment behaviour of firms. If as a result investment increases in j then there will be further incentives favouring migration from i to j and (possibly) further investment. Such a positive feedback loop may well continue until some other factor (say environmental stress) turns the balance of advantage in a different direction, and so on. In this way the socio-economic model is capable of simulating the structural changes which result in fundamental transformations in the way in which people earn their living and the very different economic environments in which the dynamics of economic activity unfold. These in turn, generate changes in employment opportunities, and land use, changes which are then analysed and displayed in map form by the graphical display component of the modelling framework.

At this stage the Crete model consists of three sectors (agriculture, industry and services) and two internal regions (the urban centres, consisting of Iraklion, Hania and Rethimnon; and the rural parts) of the island. Each of these regions is represented in the model in terms of the amount of area available for any economic activity to take place and grow, and the costs that they incur in terms of rent. The model also includes the movement of the population from one region to the other, which follows their place of employment. Finally, it allows for international influences by the inclusion of a 'rest of the world' region whose behaviour is determined exogenously. Calibration was carried out for the periods 1971–81 and 1971–90, although in practice the model was relatively invariant to calibration over these two different time periods. Once completed, and predictions checked with empirical data, it was assumed that the model represents a working representation of the underlying dynamics of the Crete economy. It was now ready to be used as a decision tool – for example, by making interventions in year 1 (say 1981) and calculating the likelihood[1] of certain environmental outcomes in year n (say 2001) through techniques such as those of risk analysis.

The central element may be seen with reference to the way our model assumes employers to behave as a result of changes in economic circumstances. It calculates the number of new jobs in each region according to how well its sectors are generating profits per unit of output and consequently expanding (or reducing) production. The actual assumptions underlying this calculation are quite complicated and are discussed in more detail elsewhere in the text and in other publications.[2] At this stage however, we are able to generate an expansion or contraction of the vacancies (V) that could potentially be filled (or the number of people losing their jobs as a result of reductions in output). This equation relates changes in vacancies as a function of relative sectorial profitability, past trends in the labour market and the structure of the labour market with respect to specific sectors and zones.

If the sector is contracting, then V_i^l is less than 0 and:

$$\frac{\partial V_i^l}{\partial t} = \alpha * J_i^l \left(\frac{P_i^l}{C_i^l} - 1 \right) - \alpha * V_i^l \tag{5.1}$$

Otherwise the sector is expanding and:

$$\frac{\partial V_i^l}{\partial t} = \alpha * J_i^l \left(\frac{P_i^l}{C_i^l} - 1 \right) * \left[1 + \varepsilon * \sum_{l'} \left(J_i^{l'} - oldJ_i^l \right) \right]$$

$$- \sigma * V_i^l * \left(\frac{0.75 * Pop_i}{\sum_{l} oldJ_i^l} - 1 \right) \tag{5.2}$$

where $oldJ_i^l$ = jobs in the previous time period,
           Pop_i = population in zone i,
           α = investment response parameter,
           $\delta V/\delta t$ = rate of change of vacancies,
           J = current jobs,
           P = prices,
           l' = other sector(s),
           ε, σ = job history response parameters.

The term with sector(s) l' are included to represent the effects of intersectoral trade, while C_i^l = costs for sector l in region i, are given by:

$$C_i^l = \sum_{l'} \sum_{j} Jcross^{l'l} * \left[P_j^{l'} + ts_i^l * d_{ij} \right] * RA_{ji}^{l'} + \frac{wage_i^l + Rent_i * space_i^l}{Pr\,y(t)_i^l} \tag{5.3}$$

where ts^l = transportation costs for a unit of l between i and j,
           d_{ij} = distance between i and j,
           $RA_{ji}^{l'}$ = relative attractivity of goods from i with respect to j,
         $Pr\,y(t)_i^l$ = labour productivity in zone i for sector l.

5.4 Scenario Development (Tourism)

Although we plan to increase the range of regions and economic sectors, the model at present consists only of two zones (rural and urban) and three sectors (agriculture, industry and services). Essentially this procedure puts rather more strain on exogenous influences (i.e. the rest of the world) than is desirable at this stage although it is arguable that the open economy nature of Crete warrants it. The particular difficulty of course is that there is no real sense in which the external sector would respond to the evolutionary behaviour of the Crete economy so that exogenous influences have to be handled differently. From our viewpoint a particularly important example of this is that of tourism, which has only begun to play a growing role in overall economic activity comparatively recently, but whose impact on the environment is certainly going to be considerable in years to come.

The way this has been dealt with is to suppose that for Europe as a whole development of tourism in the Mediterranean for a holiday has produced a growing economic 'potential'. With the technological progress of jet airliners, and the possibility of mass air transport, a certain number of 'jobs' became possible in the tourist areas. However, if there are no hotels or apartments for them to stay in, then clearly the numbers that can come are limited. If, however, some investment in tourist facilities is made which is found to be profitable, then more facilities will be developed.

In the model, we have assumed that tourism encompasses all service provision in Crete over the period under consideration (1971–2005), a rather heroic assumption but one made purely for purposes of illustration. We then suppose an 'external demand' for tourist services, and that Crete captures a fraction of this depending on its competitiveness compared to that of rivals, and also depending on the amount of tourist space available. In fact, if required, the whole process can be modelled in some detail, showing the growing 'attraction' of a destination, as its facilities develop, as well as its reputation among potential customers. Later, however, the activity may use up most of the prime tourist space, and hence begin to suffer from higher wage costs. As this happens, demand itself may begin to decline, thus leading to a decrease in profitability and the stagnation or decline of the sector.

Demand for hotel beds and accommodation will grow as long as prices are reasonable, and this will depend on the competitiveness of Crete in the market, compared to alternatives offering a similar experience. Tourist facilities will grow, and wages will rise but will be tempered by the possibilities offered in other activities in Crete. Tourism will pull labour away from traditional activities which could, for example, provide a stimulus for agricultural mechanisation, although this has not yet been explicitly modelled. The model can capture this whole process as additional tourist developments are begun, and are completed giving rise to employment, and to economic returns in the sector.

Such developments will then begin to impinge on the other sectors affecting their production characteristics as higher prices begin to be offered for non-traditional crops and other commodities. For example water consumption will undoubtedly increase and may soon start to conflict with the needs of agriculture and industry. Conversely the whole system may suffer decline if tourist demand should decrease for some reason. Perhaps fashions may change and other types of holiday become more attractive, or perhaps the supply of holiday facilities may start to outstrip demand, and so lead to a decline in prices, and hence in profitability. Recession may occur in Northern Europe and lead to reduced demand. All these scenarios may be investigated using further refinements of the model, and can be explored together with the resulting changes in land use, demand and supply of goods and services, and in the labour market.

5.4.1 The α Parameter

A key parameter in the exercise is the α parameter in equations (5.1) and (5.2), since this governs the responsiveness of investment in any sector to economic incentives. One way of handling this parameter in a scenario analysis is to assume that it reflects specific societal characteristics or attributes. For purposes of exposition we have chosen the following three with a high (H), medium (M) and low (L) weight attached to each:

- growth-oriented societal attitude,
- degree of cultural attachment,
- demographic dynamics.

A *growth-oriented societal attitude* reflects overall attitudes towards growth on the part of society as a whole. It can vary from high, resembling the stereotyped 'Western' entrepreneurial views about growth, to low, expressing similarity to societal values often held to be typical of some less-developed countries. *Cultural attachment* reflects the influence of people's cultural perceptions as influenced by factors such as family structure, history and national politics. The degree of cultural attachment can also range from high, expressing high values placed by people on traditional cultural values, to low, characterising the extreme opposite. *Demographic dynamics* refers to the level of immigration/emigration flows at constant growth rates (about 0.8% according to estimates furnished by the Blue Plan in 1989).[3] High demographic dynamism corresponds to a high value of the 'alpha' parameter and implies a high natural rate of population mobility, whereas a low value of the 'alpha' parameter assumes a low rate of population mobility.

Figure 5.3   Attributes of alternative scenarios for Crete

Attributes	AS1	AS2	AS3
Growth-oriented societal attitude	H	L	M
Degree of cultural attachment	L	H	M
Demographic dynamics	H	L	M

Figure 5.4   Scenarios for tourism

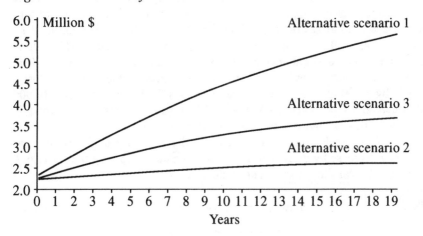

Figure 5.3 summarises the qualitative description of each alternative scenario in relation to the attributes presented above, while Figure 5.4, illustrates how the three scenarios translate into economic terms for the services sector in the island of Crete. The three curves represent the way in which demand in the services sector might increase over the 20-year time horizon for each of the three alternative scenarios that have been developed. The model then generates 'trade-off values' for the available number of jobs and land use changes, expressed in square kilometres, for each economic sector. Land use change is also spatially referenced. The trade-off values reflect environmental degradation and development growth. Environmental degradation involves factors such as land degradation, water shortages and

the vulnerability of tourism-dependent sectors in terms of lost skills and resources. Development growth refers to improved income-earning opportunities which affect proportionally the spending for goods and services in each sector of the economy.

5.4.2 Alternative Scenarios

The analysis that follows presents in detail each of the three alternative scenarios developed.

Alternative scenario 1
The 'alpha' parameter was set equal to a very high value (0.06). Such a value assumes Cretan employers to respond fast to changes in growth, showing low cultural attachment and high demographic dynamism. Table 5.1 shows the trade-offs generated for this alternative. The number of jobs in the agricultural sector in the rural areas of the island, are curtailed by almost a half, falling from 90,000 in 1981 to 48,200 in year 2001, while in the urban areas a slight increase is expected, moving up from 5,000 to 7,200. The agricultural jobs lost will be transferred either to industry (whereby 5,000 in rural areas in 1981 becomes 79,000 in 2001, and 10,000 in urban areas becomes 16,600 in 2001) or to services, most probably tourism, where a high rise is expected (from 47,000 in 1981 to 128,300 in 2001). Conversely, the service sector of the economy in the rural areas suffers a decrease by more than a half, moving down from 34,000 to 11,600 over the 20-year time span of our model run.

Table 5.1 Trade-off values of alternative scenario 1

Number of jobs (X1000)	Agriculture	Industry	Services
Rural areas	(90) 48.2	(5) 7.9	(34) 11.6
Urban areas	(5) 7.2	(10) 16.6	(47) 128.3

Land use change (km^2)	Agriculture	Industry	Services
Rural areas	(1,085) 578	(17) 23	(69) 23
Urban areas	(44) 86	(32) 49	(95) 256

* Values in brackets refer to year 1981, while the rest refer to year 2001.

Land use changes also take place. Agricultural land decreases in rural areas moving down from 1,085 to 578 square kilometres, while it appears to double in the urban areas. Some land is also taken over by industry, rising from 23 to 49 square kilometres and from 17 to 32 square kilometres in rural and urban areas respectively over the 1981–2001 period. The most dramatic land use change occurs in the service sector, moving up from 95 square kilometres in 1981 to 256 square kilometres in 2001 in the urban areas, while decreasing from 69 to 23 square kilometres in the rural areas. The land use changes generated by the model were also given spatial location (Figure 5.5). Changes are shown with reference to a baseline tourism suitability map of 1981 (Figure 5.6). On the baseline map in Figure 5.5 four classes were distinguished on the basis of several criteria (Kazaklis, Perez-Trejo and Kazana, 1992). These criteria include landscape characteristics such as elevation, water availability, vegetation, road densities, proximity to the sea, and proximity to airports and others. The same criteria were used to identify the most likely spatial location where the changes indicated by the dynamic model might actually occur.

Figure 5.5   Land use units in Crete

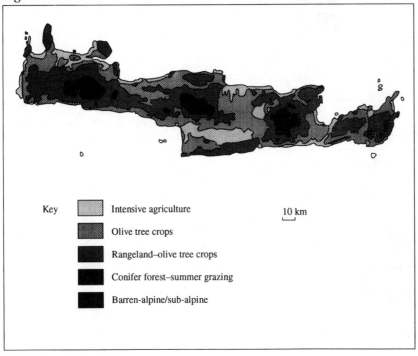

Figure 5.6   Tourism suitability map

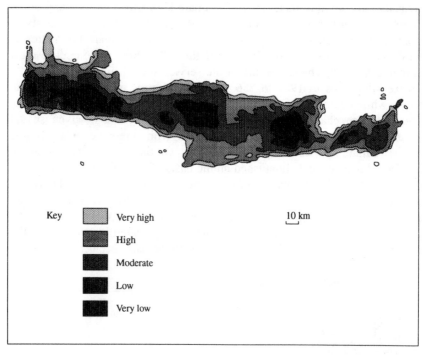

Table 5.2 Trade-off values of alternative scenario 2

Number of jobs (X1000)	Agriculture	Industry	Services
Rural areas	(90) 90	(5) 5	(34) 34
Urban areas	(5) 5	(10) 11	(47) 52

Land use change (km²)	Agriculture	Industry	Services
Rural areas	(1,085)1,080	(17) 17	(69) 69
Urban areas	(44) 47	(32) 33	(95) 105

* Values in brackets refer to year 1981, while the rest refer to year 2001.

Alternative scenario 2

In this scenario the 'α' value was equated to a very low value (0.006). Such a value assumes Cretan people are rather reluctant to respond to changes in growth, being highly attached to their culture and having low demographic dynamism. The trade-off values show very small changes over time as can be observed from Table 5.2. The number of jobs shows a slight increase in the industrial sector (by 1,000) and in the service sector (by 5,000) in the urban areas. Land use change follows a similar pattern. Some land is taken by services (10 square kilometres), industry (1 square kilometre) and agriculture (5 square kilometres) in the urban areas, while the agricultural sector loses some land in the rural areas (5 square kilometres). Since the land use change generated by running this alternative scenario is very small, no map was produced to locate it spatially.

Alternative scenario 3

Between the extreme alternative scenarios 1 and 2 a third alternative was developed by setting the value of the 'alpha' parameter equal to 0.03. This value implies a moderate response on the part of Cretan employers to economic changes, as well as moderate values for cultural attachment and demographic dynamism. Table 5.3 shows the trade-off values for the third alternative scenario.

Table 5.3   Trade-off values of alternative scenario 3

Number of jobs (X1000)	Agriculture	Industry	Services
Rural areas	(90) 80.8	(5) 6.7	(34) 30.1
Urban areas	(5) 5.2	(10) 13.0	(47) 79

Land use change (km^2)	Agriculture	Industry	Services
Rural areas	(1,085) 969	(17) 20	(69) 60
Urban areas	(44) 62	(32) 38	(95) 158

* Values in brackets refer to year 1981, while the rest refer to year 2001.

It may be seen that the agricultural and the service sectors contract in the rural areas with respect to the number of jobs (800 and 39,000 respectively). A similar pattern is shown for land use change in these areas and sectors. The urban agricultural and service sectors appear to expand by

200 and 32,000 jobs respectively. The same holds true for industry in both regions, rural and urban, with an expected increase of 1,700 and 3,000 respectively. Land use change follows a similar pattern.

5.4.3   Discussion of Results

All three alternative scenarios are possible in the next 20 years. However, the third scenario appears to us most realistic, having regard to background information about the culture, history, politics and natural resources of the island economy of Crete.   Allbaugh (1953), for example, has described Crete as a place that has suffered centuries of conquest, wars and revolutions with traditional attitudes that imply self-sufficiency and self-defence, and little sign of collectivist values on the part of individuals. Although the last 40 years have been years of peace and although some development has taken place, it may well be that these overall attitudes of the Cretan people have not changed significantly. Because of this the high growth scenario (AS1) appears to us unlikely, while the low growth scenario (AS2) is probably ruled out by general exigencies of economic change.

Figure 5.7   Projected expansion of tourism in the year 2001

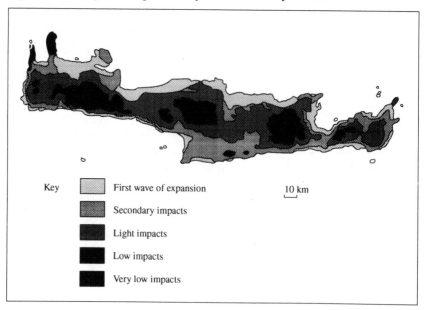

Provided the third scenario (AS3) unfolds in the way we predict over the coming years, tourism (expressed within the service sector) is expected to increase by a considerable amount causing substantial changes in land use patterns (Figure 5.7). This is threatening for both the urban and the rural areas. Tourism suitability class 1, which is considered highly preferable by tourists, will extend around the urban areas taking over land from agricultural uses (mainly annual crops, fruit crops and olive trees). This will then have a number of associated effects. Urbanisation will increase, while the rural areas will be drained of human resources, hence having a significant impact on land degradation, mainly through the abandonment of traditional land conservation techniques (terraces). Water requirements will change with probably a significant impact in the urban areas, as it has already been documented that water consumption will increase following the increase of tourism (Grenon and Batisse, 1989), and since resources are scarce there is likely to be a significant water allocation problem. Environmental impacts will probably also be observed through cultural changes in family structure and other features of general life style. Last, but no less important to mention, are dangers to tourism-dependent sectors, whereby traditional skills and related capabilities may well be irretrievably lost.

5.5   RISK ANALYSIS

The technique of risk analysis is not new, having been used in a variety of decision-making applications, such as, for example, the evaluation of simulated water-management strategies in reservoir systems (Hirsch, 1978) and the evaluation of empirically determined exposures to carcinogens (Whyte and Burton, 1980). However, in a more recent paper Cincotta and Perez-Trejo (1990) suggest that it could also have an important role to play in helping to deal with problems of natural resource degradation especially when combined with simulation modelling of natural systems. They argue that it compares favourably to other techniques such as those of cost/benefit analysis or straightforward biologically-based simulation models, used on their own. The former suffer from having to reduce everything to an economic calculus which is often far too crude, while the latter do not provide a framework within which strategies can be easily compared.

The way the method works is to start with a simulation model of the system under examination and to define 'acceptance limits' for important decision quantities associated with its expected future evolution. For example, in wildlife conservation managers often recognise biological and sociological population limits below which species are in danger of extinction. Similarly 'in grazing and vegetation management there are limits that correspond to plant composition thresholds at which vegetation changes rapidly to communities of less desirable species. Managers often find it difficult to restore the original plant compositional state, or [anticipate that] to do so would prove prohibitively costly'.[4] By randomly varying key model parameters and running the model a sufficiently large number of times, it is possible to estimate the probability that the decision quantity will fall below the specified acceptance limit. This information can then be used for decision-making purposes. Cincotta and Perez-Trejo illustrate the method by means of a (fictitious) case comparison of two candidate technologies for agricultural production in a poor area. The random variable is annual rainfall, while the risk analysis is carried out for a range of decision quantities such as output, soil erosion and the sustainability of fisheries.

The authors claim that risk analysis has a number of advantages as a decision support tool. To begin with the method is perfectly general and can be used in a wide variety of contexts. Secondly it encompasses the whole system in question in an interdisciplinary fashion, and so does not suffer the drawbacks associated with partial analysis. Indeed it specifically encourages dialogue between natural science and social research to the ultimate benefit of both. Finally it has the merit of increasing the potential for stakeholder participation in decision making, for example by facilitating discussion of acceptance limits and allowable risks associated with these. It may easily be seen, therefore, that these are precisely the features of decision making that we have already highlighted in this book as necessary for the effective understanding of, and intervention in, evolutionary socio-economic and natural systems.

5.6 EMPLOYMENT FORECASTS

The first scenario run extends the Crete model to the year 2001 and focuses on jobs expected to be created in the tourism sector over the period 1981–2001. What we have done is to randomly generate values for external demand for tourism in each of the years 1981–2001 and to run the model one hundred times for each set of demand values. Doing this generates the results given in Figure 5.8 below. It combines the two scenarios as a set of expected annual job projections for the specified period. It may be seen that the projections vary from c.66,000 to c.74,000 jobs. If the planning authority has anticipated a growth rate of 2% per annum, the risk analysis shows that it is likely to be correct only 32% of the time. Accordingly we should expect it to revise its growth-rate estimates downwards if it continues to accept the validity of the underlying model over the period in question. Alternatively the authority may wish to explore further the growth constraints that are implicit in the model's parameters (see below).

Figure 5.8   Expansion of tourism (1981–2001)

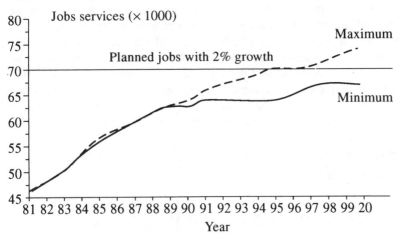

Finally it is also worth noting that job projections in tourism are relatively insensitive to external demand factors on the basis of these scenario runs, a result which would appear to support the validity of the overall model.

A second scenario experiment was then conducted, this time with annual projected data on jobs in tourism assuming a rate of growth of 2% per annum – i.e. consistent with the overall 20-year target estimated above. Again randomly generated values for external demand were used and the computer runs assessed to show the probability, in any year, of available jobs not reaching the level of projected estimates. The risk analysis showed that only in 2.3% of the runs did job estimates fall below projected levels, a value that would appear to vindicate the target growth rates.

A series of experiments was then made on variability in the α parameter. In this case α was varied from 0.006 to 0.06 (10 times) leading to projected job variation from 52,000 to 128,000 (2.3 times). A wide range of estimates of this key parameter makes comparatively little difference to future job estimates. However, performing a simple risk analysis shows that any uncertainty in the parameter generates a much higher risk of failure than that due to external demand uncertainty. Thus 35% of the runs with a variable α projected job totals of less than 70,000. It would appear therefore more important for the planning authority to be clear about α than about likely future demand for tourism in its forecasting activities.

5.7   THE NATURAL SYSTEM

Finally let us explore briefly how the inclusion of the natural system may be handled in our analysis, using the case of water management as an exemplar. What we have done here is to link relative water shortage in any sector/region to productivity, which in turn affects supply and therefore costs. As relative costs change across sectors and regions there will be an impact on both investment and demographic behaviour, which in turn will affect future exploitation of limited water resources. In this way, albeit rather crudely, it is possible to tie the evolution of the economic system to that of the natural system. Using a very simple set of equations this may be described in a little more detail as follows.

Let the dynamics of productivity $\left(Pr\, y_i^l(t) \right)$ for each sector (l) and region (i) be given by the equation:

$$\frac{\delta\ Pr\, y_i^l}{\delta t} = Pr\, y_i^l(t) \; * \; \left\{ 1 - \left(\frac{UsedLand_i^l}{AvailableLand_i^l} \right) \right\} * \left\{ 1 - \left(\frac{WaterUse_i^l}{AvailableWater_i^l} \right) \right\} \quad (5.4)$$

$$\underbrace{\phantom{\left\{ 1 - \left(\frac{UsedLand_i^l}{AvailableLand_i^l} \right) \right\}}}_{\text{Marginality of Land}} \qquad \underbrace{\phantom{\left\{ 1 - \left(\frac{WaterUse_i^l}{AvailableWater_i^l} \right) \right\}}}_{\text{Water Scarcity}}$$

This (Ricardian) formulation assumes that productivity for a given sector l in region i is diminished as the activity in the sector begins to take up more land and extends over into land that is less productive. In a similar way, as the water used by the economic activity begins to exceed the amount of water that is actually available, productivity for that sector in that region begins to decrease. Water scarcity then affects the model through its impact on productivity by reducing the supply of products in the sector and region through the productivity term in the equation

$$SUPPLY_i^l = Jobs_i^l \; * \; Price_i^l \; * \; Pr\, y(t)_i^l \qquad (5.5)$$

which in turn affects costs of production in the sector and region where it occurs, as reflected in the portion of the equation where fixed unit costs are a function of productivity:

$$C_i^l = \sum_{l'} \sum_j Jcross^{l'l} * \left[P_j^{l'} + ts_i^l * d_{ij} \right] * RA_{ji}^{l'} + \frac{wage_i^l + Rent_i * space_i^l}{Pr\, y(t)_i^l} \qquad (5.6)$$

$$\underbrace{\phantom{\sum_{l'} \sum_j Jcross}}_{\text{Input Costs}} \qquad \underbrace{\phantom{\frac{wage_i^l + Rent_i}{Pr\, y}}}_{\text{Fixed Costs}}$$

Note: This equation is the same as equation (5.3).

Figure 5.9   Water-use scenario

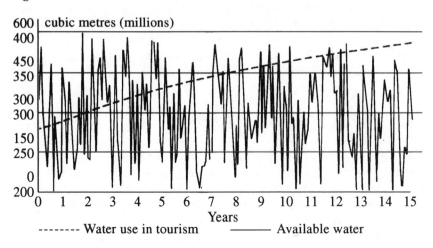

-------- Water use in tourism   ———— Available water

To illustrate how the methodology can be used to explore the effects of policy on the environment, successive runs of the model, including the dynamics of water scarcity, were then made to estimate the risk of water scarcity in the tourism sector around the city of Hania, as illustrated in Figure 5.9 which shows the results of a run of the model with varying water supply to the service sector in the urban zone of Hania. In this case the socio-economic model had been calibrated over the period 1971–90. The results show that the likelihood of water shortage evolves from 20% in 1990 to 85% in 2005. This calculated value of risk is not necessarily the *actual* water shortage that might be experienced by tourists in Hania in the year 2005, but reflects rather a measure of the difficulty that the industry will encounter in supplying water to an ever increasing tourist demand. If tourists continue to visit the area then additional water will need to be imported to meet local demand, and the costs will be passed on to the customer. However, if the cost of water supply begins to increase holiday prices, this is likely then to have a significant impact on the attractiveness of Hania as a tourist destination, and on the overall profitability of tourism in Crete.

In addition if the tourism sector is as successful as this scenario assumes it might be in the next 15 years, then we can expect an increase in competition for scarce water resources between different productive sectors, especially large users such as agriculture. The 85% risk estimate is indicative of the likelihood of increased water conflicts which will tend to resolve themselves through the market mechanism unless there is policy intervention. In a market-driven economy the sector that generates most profits tends to be most successful in securing water supplies at the expense of other less profitable economic activities. This may have severe consequences on the long-term sustainability of each of the regions affected. Most importantly, it may affect access to water thereby affecting the quality of life more generally. It is in these ways that the inclusion of a simple water resource submodel can help the policy-making process.

5.8   SOME CONCLUDING POINTS

The objective of this chapter has been one of extending the modelling approach outlined in Chapter 4 to illustrate its uses as a decision tool. We have carried this out by means of a simplified 2-region, 3-sector model of the Mediterranean island of Crete calibrated over the period 1971–91 and then used to develop scenarios to the year 2001. In this way we have tried to show that considering the spatial dimension in a direct way is a necessity, if we are to increase our understanding of the process of desertification. However, analysing the spatial dynamics of living systems represents an enormous challenge and one, arguably, that most scientific disciplines have avoided up until recently. For example, Perez-Trejo (1989) shows that even though geographic information systems (GIS) tools have made significant progress in helping to describe the spatial dimension of environmental problems, they still fall short where it comes to addressing the conceptual and methodological aspects of processes which drive the spatial dynamics of the underlying systems.

A clear case in point here is the treatment of hierarchy. Thus Figure 5.2 suggests a much finer hierarchical scale than is encompassed by the model itself, which is essentially a twofold micro/macro hierarchy.[5] To some extent we hope to achieve a better correspondence using the incorporation of the DRU analysis outlined in Chapter 6, but nevertheless we are very conscious of the limited progress we have made in capturing the evolutionary properties of systems like this. How to engage meaningfully with the realities of changing socio-economic systems (as well as their natural resource underpinnings) is clearly going to become, we believe, an important agenda item for the future, and one for which there will be no easy answers. The very rudimentary models discussed here are therefore to be seen as only a very preliminary attempt to come to terms with a very complicated set of practical and theoretical issues. In other words we have seen that the Crete model can generate simulated migration and employment results which correspond quite closely to real data. However, we should stress that these, rather crude, scenarios have been presented for purposes of illustration only – that is, to show how this type of evolutionary modelling can be used to inform issues of practical policy.

NOTES

1　We use the term 'likelihood' rather than 'probability' to reflect the dependence of the exercise on a model which is still at a very crude stage of development.
2　See Appendix I and Chapter 4. See also, for example, Perez-Trejo et al. (1993a).
3　See Blue Plan (1992).
4　See Cincotta and Perez-Trejo (1990), p. 193.
5　We are grateful to Don Funnell for drawing our attention to this point.

6. An Agenda for the Future

6.1 INTRODUCTION

Our objective in this final chapter is to bring together the lessons learned as a result of the modelling simulations outlined in Chapters 4 and 5, and to place these lessons within the overall context of systems thinking outlined in the opening chapters. It will be recalled from Chapter 1 that the book has been written as a contribution to the practical management of sustainable ecosystems, particularly with reference to those of developing countries, although it also makes some rather more fundamental statements about the scope and nature of the scientific method.

In the opening chapters we outlined two basic deficiencies inherent in much of conventional policy research. These are first, the barriers to integrated management practices that result from narrow disciplinary boundaries. Problems like those of desertification for example, are not such that they can be meaningfully understood or analysed from the standpoint of any one discipline such as geography or economics. Rather they result from the total interaction of human and natural systems over long periods of time. Nevertheless, there is a strong tendency for disciplinary perspectives to prevail in much contemporary policy analysis, dependent, of course, upon the disciplinary biases of whatever research team is conducting the enquiry. The inevitable result is that most analysis is partial and so does not in general capture the complexity of ecosystem evolution.

The second problem is the related one that most established disciplines, and their associated models, suffer from having an unduly mechanistic perspective on the evolution of ecosystems. There is always a (sometimes unconscious) desire to discover *the* fundamental model which encapsulates *all* ecosystem behaviour over *all* time periods. Such a deterministic model, of course, does not exist. Indeed no creative, and hence unpredictable, system could be described in this way.

It is for these reasons that we have spent some considerable time laying out the conceptual basis of our approach. Chapter 2 began by defining the concept of a system independent of the context of its use, an essential step, we felt, in our overall argument since all too often the word 'system' is used loosely in the relevant literature. In this chapter particular attention was paid to the behaviour, and general characteristics of, open (living) systems as opposed to closed (physical) systems. In particular the discussion focused on their broad evolutionary properties and how they may be explored analytically.

Chapter 3 then went on to depict economic systems as open evolutionary systems having the properties discussed in Chapter 2. Our main reason for writing this chapter was to provide an analytical basis for the subsequent modelling work discussed in Chapters 4 and 5, but an important subsidiary reason was to deal with our criticisms of conventional models set out in the first chapter and outlined above. This has been done by means of a critique of modern Schumpeterian literature dealing with the subject of economic evolution. Despite the great contribution this literature has made, it has been unable to provide an adequate modelling schema useful for our purposes – that is, one that can function effectively as a decision tool (or set of tools) which integrates the co-evolutionary behaviour of the natural system.

Finally Chapters 4 and 5 set out an account of our preliminary modelling activities, first with respect to the Senegal model and second with respect to that of Crete. Chapter 4 describes the Senegal model as an exemplar of an evolutionary economic system and outlines the important properties such a model should possess. Chapter 5 goes on to apply these ideas to a similar model (that of the Island of Crete) and shows how such a model can be used as a decision tool to explore specific policy scenarios, in this case using tourism as an example. In this chapter too we have combined the use of risk analysis with the Crete model in order to show how the implications of a particular policy may be explored with benefit to all the stakeholders who are liable to be affected by that policy decision.

6.2 THE NATURE OF KNOWLEDGE

Before describing in detail the broad lessons to be learned from the book as a whole, it is useful to return to an argument which has been made on a number of occasions throughout the text. This concerns the nature of knowledge and the most suitable means for its search, validation, processing and use. Our broad aim throughout the text has been one of developing appropriate decision tools for natural-resource management in complex evolutionary situations and our approach has, therefore, emphasised the contingent nature of knowledge – that is, how knowledge only really takes on complete meaning in relation to the context in which it is being used.[1]

Now in terms of conventional knowledge-seeking practices this is actually quite a radical claim to make since it runs counter to popularly accepted canons of scientific enquiry. Nevertheless the claim is fundamental to our overall argument and needs therefore to be carefully spelt out even though we have already touched on it briefly at the end of Chapter 2, and at other points. The argument runs as follows. The most important distinction between physical systems, on the one hand, and natural and social systems on the other, is that the former do not evolve. Or at least they evolve so slowly that for all practical purposes they can be treated as non-evolutionary. Since they do not evolve they can be subjected to experimentation designed to uncover their properties and behaviour, and the success of such experimentation is determined by the accuracy of derived predictions. 'Knowledge' related to such systems can therefore be held to be universally true and applicable over time and space.

Natural/social systems, conversely, have the important property that they constantly experience co-evolutionary change and so cannot be defined parametrically in the same sense. All we can reasonably claim is that their parameters (which give definition to their structures) change more slowly than their variables. To give a stark example, while it is likely that Newton's gravitational constant has not changed since it was first discovered in the eighteenth century, there is no sense in which we can identify a similar constant parameter for any specific ecosystem as it existed at that time. What this means is that we can really only apply the 'scientific method' in the formal sense, to the analysis of systems whose parameters remain relatively stable – that is, physical systems or biological systems whose structures tend to remain reasonably stable. In the latter case we could, for example, be 'scientific' about the behaviour of a particular kind of cancer cell in a well-defined context, whereas it would be extremely hard to take the same experimental view about a complex watershed of 2,000 hectares in the south of India. It therefore also means that we need a rather different approach to the analysis of both natural systems and social systems – an approach which allows us to capture their evolutionary reality without at the same time imprisoning them in the pseudo-science of an artificial determinism.

This point of view is certainly not the prevailing one. Conventional wisdom is still very dependent upon what has been described as the 'pipeline view' of knowledge acquisition, validation and use (Clark, 1987, 1995) despite a critique that goes back certainly to the late 1960s.[2] Under this view a normative distinction is made between institutions and organisations whose role is to search for new knowledge on the one hand, and those whose function it is to translate that knowledge into economic production on the other. The resultant division of labour is hierarchical and conforms, in a sense, to the 'mass production' manufacturing paradigm we discussed at the end of Chapter 3. University departments and state-funded research institutes carry out pure research according to canons of objectivity determined by the cognitive authority of peer review. The knowledge that results from this activity is then drawn upon as and when needed by a productive sector which has quite a different agenda, that of making money from the sale of goods and services. Whether it refers to the natural or the social sciences makes no real difference. The market will draw upon the technological resources it needs as and when necessary.

The reason why the term 'pipeline' is used is due to the recognition that in practice there is a continuum between knowledge search and knowledge use and therefore that it is more realistic to postulate the innovation process as one of knowledge flows through a 'pipeline' which has basic research activity at one end and knowledge embodied as useful products at the other (see Figure 6.1). At the basic research end resources are allocated to 'basic' science having only the greater understanding of nature as its objective. Some of the resultant knowledge, however, has potential economic value and so further resources are then 'applied' to this knowledge to enhance its technological power. Finally, once the new technology shows good commercial promise resources are given to 'develop' the innovation to its ultimate commercial form.

Figure 6.1   Simple pipeline model

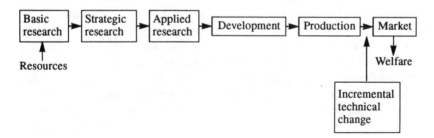

The research sequence – basic, applied, development – is sometimes extended to basic, 'strategic', applied, development, 'incremental'. The addition of 'incremental' is introduced to take account of the fact that new technologies are never static but rather evolve into new forms as a result of economic pressures over time. The distinction of 'strategic', from 'basic', is made to take account of the existence of fundamental research which is nevertheless funded because it has some broad mission orientation. The research financed through the Human Genome Project, for example, is 'strategic' in this sense.

Our argument in this book, however, is that such a view of knowledge hierarchy is consistent neither with the reality of evolutionary systems nor with the underlying nature of knowledge itself. On the first point, and as Rosen (1987) has pointed out in relation to natural ecologies, no creative system could survive if its access to useful information were constrained in this way. And if that is so with natural systems how much more must it be the case with complex socio-economic systems whose creativity depends in a fundamental sense on speedy access to, and the efficient processing of, information flows that are themselves evolving in a complex manner at ever increasing rates? There is nowadays so much information being produced, in so many different forms and at such speeds, that even with the advent of modern information technologies it is becoming ever more difficult for the typical 'economic agent' to cope.

In fact the idea of the centralised knowledge source (the 'universitatis') as the *main* avenue for productive knowledge is increasingly seen to be both inefficient and misleading. Instead it is gradually becoming recognised that to a growing extent useful knowledge in complex systems is context dependent. This being so, there is a premium on the development of tools which allow the economically productive organisation to access such knowledge efficiently. And those concerned with environmentally sensitive development planning are not exempt. But that is easier said than done since there are often considerable difficulties in coming to agreement about the true nature of the underlying system that is being planned.

A writer who has done as much as anyone to clarify this point is a systems ecologist, Bob Rosen, whose original background lay in the analysis of complex biological systems, but who has also tried to show that similar metaphors are applicable to the dynamical behaviour of socio-economic systems as well. He too takes the view that conventional science works best with physical systems. Conversely in the case of living systems (ecologies) that are creative, and as a result experience evolution of internal structures, we need an experimental approach that allows us to capture the inevitable indeterminism of their behaviour. Such an approach needs above all to avoid constraining our analysis of the system under investigation by presuppositions about its 'true nature' and in particular, that of imagining that it can be modelled deterministically.

Indeed much of development planning literature, he argues, shows evidence of a lack of clarity (fuzziness) surrounding many of the associated concepts. Not only have analysts no clear idea about what constitutes 'development' (they are often actually incompatible and contradictory), 'even among those who happen to share the same views as to the ends of development, there are similarly incompatible views as to the means by which the ends can be attained'.[3]   Similar general views have been expressed more recently by Thompson (1993). But, Rosen goes on, if 'so many distinct and contradictory views ... can be held by (so many) able people ... [then] ... a first step in dealing with such concepts is to try to identify and remove the source of the fuzziness'.[4] And an important source in his view, is that different analysts 'live intellectually' in a variety of different 'analytical worlds' where the underlying concepts used often have different meanings to each analyst. Sometimes, unfortunately, they are not fully understood by the analysts themselves even in terms of their own 'world'. However, if we begin to separate out these worlds and characterise them unambiguously, then we shall have made an important first step in clearing up much of the confusion.

So how is this to be done? Rosen's method is to abstract from the Newtonian mechanics which underlie most models of system behaviour (including system dynamics), and in particular to introduce the notion of 'anticipation'. In relation to any economic system there are potentially an infinite array of models that can describe its evolutionary properties. This being so, there is a need for analysts to enter into dialogue with each other with the objective of reaching a consensus on which one, or ones, best describe it. A rather different approach may be found in some of the recent literature on the 'social shaping' of technology where a number of writers have begun to investigate the many ways in which the actual practice of knowledge search is conditioned by various kinds of cognitive, social and economic interests. Edge (1988), for example, argues that it is 'becoming increasingly clear that ... the factors influencing the rate, directions and specific forms of technical change are *social as well as technical*. The evidence for this is overwhelming: economic, cultural, political and organisational factors – all of which we subsume in the term "social" – have been shown to shape technological change'.[5] Showing how this is the case in the context of a range of technologies/industries such as numerically controlled machine tools, robotics and missile guidance systems, he goes on to suggest a practical policy agenda that emphasises the creation of effective networks that enable different knowledge sources to work effectively together in circumstances that will usually vary widely across both industry and technology.

More recently still, Gremmen (1993) has shown how much of the knowledge required for economic production is usually acquired as an integral aspect of the production process itself and therefore denies the primacy of any particular type of scientific knowledge. Knowledge nowadays has become so much part and parcel of all types of practical activity that its pursuit, processing, validation and dissemination takes place at all levels of the 'pipeline'. In similar vein Gibbons (ed.) (1994) contains a series of papers that have as a common thread the distinction between 'mode 1' and 'mode 2' types of knowledge, the latter being the kinds of context-related knowledge that is increasingly coming to dominate the picture as a whole. Hicks (1995) shows how Japanese firms encourage their scientists to publish research results in academic journals as part of a process of knowledge creation that enables firms to 'trade' technology more successfully than they might otherwise be able to do. In this way, and in others, the Japanese national innovation system blurs the traditional institutional division of scientific labour and encourages a significant element of cooperation across competitive firm behaviour, cooperation that is encouraged in order to enhance external economic benefits for the macroeconomic system as a whole.

In an attempt to synthesise these ideas more formally, Clark and Juma (1992) have used information theory as their starting point and linked this to evolutionary epistemology.[6] In this way they differentiate information from knowledge in a formal sense, and also incidentally show homologies with modern evolutionary traditions in other disciplines (e.g. developmental biology). Information is treated entropically as a kind of technological 'potential' that only becomes useful knowledge under specific contextual conditions. An important aspect of this is the notion of temporal hierarchy. Units of production and other economic actors are continuously being bombarded by new information which they will accept and utilise through an evolutionary process which depends upon a sort of 'credibility dynamics'. New information becomes acceptable knowledge through a process that depends fundamentally upon the cognitive, economic and other interests of the relevant actors and upon their power to actually put their awakening perceptions into action. A key determinant is therefore the ability to create institutional forms that have the capacity to orchestrate the process efficiently, a capacity that seems to be most effective in the case of East Asian models of innovation.

However, a problem with the 'social shaping of technology' literature is that while it is suggestive, it does not really deal with the practical business of policy advice. How in practice are policy makers in industry and government to find a way through the complex web of potentially useful information so as to achieve their economic and social objectives? It is on this crucial point that we believe the approach of Rosen to be particularly valuable. In order to deal with the wide array of potential models which in a sense 'compete' for 'cognitive space' with respect to any system, he constructs a model world in which time trajectories are allowed to move faster than 'real time', but where the real system (S) and the model system (M) are coupled in a policy sense through an effector system (E) (Figure 6.2). He then formalises the analysis by allowing informational feedback from E to M depending upon whether the trajectory of M is held to be 'desirable' or not. Notice that since $S + M + E$ is in total an anticipatory system (S^*), the M trajectory will always tend to forecast that of S, although the forecast will never be perfect unless M is a perfect model. We know of course that that can never be the case because S is an evolutionary system in the strict sense that the future is unknown. However, by couching the problem in terms of *anticipatory* systems Rosen opens up much more clearly the nature of the potential confusions that arise typically in development planning. Each analyst, or *analytical ideology*, has his/her (its) own social construction of reality which guides the policy questions asked and the answers that are ideologically acceptable. Rosen's argument is that at least the recognition of this fact should help to clear (some of) the intellectual baggage that obscures the policy process.

Figure 6.2   An anticipatory system

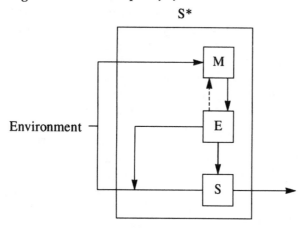

Of course, we all know examples of such ideological confusion. Economists are well known for seeing any particular issue in terms of resource allocation and the price mechanism. What usually differentiates them from a policy standpoint is the position they take up on 'market failure' in relation to that issue. Those on the 'right' tend to want to believe that a 'market solution' is the better option, whereas those on the 'left' will tend to favour intervention on the part of some central authority to correct 'market failure'. Their 'worlds' are predetermined in this narrow, ideological sense. Similar differentiation occurs across disciplines. For example, on issues of environmental degradation, physical geographers will not see the problem in terms of the efficiency of the price system but will tend rather to concentrate on purely physical processes such as climatic changes and soil and water stress. Political scientists will eschew both in favour of an analysis concentrating upon power structures. Finally it should be noted that such social construction goes well beyond intra- and interdisciplinary battles, but relates more widely to strongly held views on the part of many powerful and highly motivated pressure groups. As Thompson (1993) has pointed out in graphic detail, the passion with which rival adherents typically cling to their respective 'worlds' can potentially waste many billions of dollars. It is in this profound sense that policy analysis is not a costless exercise, illustrating clearly the need for better decision tools in the policy-making process as a whole.

6.3   ENFRANCHISING THE STAKEHOLDER

It is for this reason that the models explored in Chapters 4 and 5 should only be viewed as heuristics, as temporary and revisable 'cognitive spectacles' with which to glimpse the inner reality of socio-economic and natural systems that are changing their structures continuously. In a sense the search for knowledge itself is an evolutionary process, working in parallel with the underlying reality of the processes it is trying to comprehend. However, this relative impermanence does not mean that modelling is a futile endeavour. On the contrary, unless we have some representation to work off, our analysis is bound to be ineffective. This is especially the case because system interpretation will always vary with stakeholder perception of interests, as we argue above. There is now a growing literature on the role of stakeholder interests in policy determination and since, as we have argued above, all knowledge is contingent, there is endless room for differing interpretations of model prediction. What our complex systems approach does, however, is to begin to provide the basis for dialogue between such interests with a view to ultimate conflict resolution. Let us explore this point a little further.

According to Long and Long (eds) (1992) and Leeuwis (1993) the social actors (stakeholders) in any economic system actually engage in a continuous process of 'reality construction'.[7] There is no need to postulate *any* external reality *a priori* since that reality is in a perpetual state of negotiation and renegotiation amongst the stakeholders themselves. Indeed since each stakeholder has his own unique notion of what reality is, this is in practice the only way to proceed. In a series of recent papers Stephen Biggs and his colleagues at the School of Development Studies, University of East Anglia, UK, have also been exploring the problem of stakeholder interests in relation to the introduction of technology in rural areas, a problem which they believe is much more common than conventionally realised. For example, they have shown how the issue of rural mechanisation is very much context dependent – that is, in the sense that the success of technologies depends crucially upon the socio-economic and ecological setting within which the technologies are set to work.

A useful set of examples of the essentially contingent nature of technological change is provided by Gass and Biggs (1993) where the authors give a number of instances of pieces of machinery working well in one location but not at all in others (e.g. Kinsey and Ahmed's (1983) comparison of the successful introduction of toolbars in West Africa with practically no success in rural East Africa). At one level the reasons for this are fairly clear. Mechanisation is not just a purely 'technical' phenomenon. Rather it should be seen in holistic terms involving 'historical, political, social and institutional dimensions'.[8] At an operational level, however, this still leaves the issue unresolved. How should decisions be reached about the choice of new technologies and their introduction into a region when there are big differences in stakeholder perceptions of relative gains and losses that are expected to arise?

Gass and Biggs (1993) suggest the use of a modified version of the original Tinbergen framework for economic policy analysis. Essentially the method works as follows. Let us suppose that there are a range of possible courses of action which could be taken to deal with any specific problem. These are placed as columns on a matrix, the rows of which identify the various stakeholders who have an interest in policy outcomes. Each box in the matrix then provides a qualitative assessment of the decision payoff to the relevant stakeholder for a given policy decision and hence the matrix provides a decision tool to assist the policy maker both in coming to a final decision and in improving success in implementation. A similar approach is taken by Chambers and his colleagues when they promote Participatory Rural Appraisal (PRA) methods for socio-economic change in the Third World.[9]

While we are thoroughly supportive of these approaches (and others like them),[10] we would argue nevertheless that a further step is normally necessary in policy analysis, namely, the need for a common 'language of discourse' which will enable stakeholders to play a more central role both in the decision itself and in its implementation. By this we mean that stakeholders themselves, or their representatives, are provided with appropriate tools of analysis for holistic choice. While a stakeholder matrix certainly highlights the gainers and losers (and hence permits better dialogue amongst stakeholders), it does not provide an account of the underlying processes that characterise the system under analysis. In other words it permits opportunities to exist for disagreements about the very nature of the system itself, and to that extent therefore, obfuscates and prevents clear discussion of the issues involved.

The modelling exercise that we have introduced is precisely an attempt to deal with this deficiency. It should be seen as part of an integrated evolutionary framework which focuses on defining the system in question hierarchically in terms of processes that have specific spatial and temporal reference. In this way a conceptual model is developed from empirical observation linking process to pattern, a model which provides a holistic account of structural change. Thus the model is both a research and a decision tool. The research entails identification of hierarchical levels based on the specifics of temporal and spatial scales at which these processes operate, hence enabling the analyst to improve his capacity to explore the complex ways in which such processes might interact to generate observed patterns. At the same time the model becomes an essential account of the system itself and so allows an element of objective reality to play a part in the decision-making process. Although each stakeholder may have his own perception of his interests he has still to negotiate these with his peers using a common model as the basis for discussion.

6.4 ENDOGENISING THE ENVIRONMENT

A closely related property of our approach is its capacity to begin capturing impacts on, and effects of, environmental changes. Traditional model building starts by defining the system under consideration in terms of its structural characteristics. As we have already pointed out these are represented by system parameters which are assumed not to change over the time period of investigation and can therefore be 'estimated' by conventional statistical techniques which distinguish sharply between a 'parameter' and a 'variable'. In order to make such analysis manageable it is usually necessary to define the system fairly narrowly, that is, to render 'exogenous' influences which play a small role (it is assumed) in system behaviour or (more usually) which cannot easily be measured. For example, the practice of exogenising technological factors is a widespread case in point.

The problem is, of course, that it is precisely those factors rendered exogenous which turn out to have most practical importance. In particular the range of impacts on the natural system (usually labelled the 'environment') are often so considerable that unless they are anticipated, and remedial action taken, irreversible degradation can occur. Using a very simple water model in Chapter 5 we showed how this could be handled in a risk analysis setting. More generally, however, environmental factors are endogenised by linking a broader sub-model on landscape response to the generic model and permitting feedback linkages, as is currently being done in further elaborations of the Crete model.[11]

The method used is to start by characterising the economic system in terms of grid squares of 'suitability' for each economic sector. For the island of Crete these are approximately 5 sq. km. in area. Each grid square is then defined in terms of physiography, elevation, soil characteristics and proximity to amenities such as transportation facilities or airports. The suitabilities are then used as a 'knowledge base' to predict where each economic activity will unfold in the future, based upon critical spatial requirements. Each economic sector is given spatial dimension in a real sense, linking changes in land-use patterns generated by the model, to specific locations and environmental attributes.

The final step is then to calculate the actual environmental impact of specific socio-economic developments. The way this is being done is to divide Crete into desertification response units (DRUs) by means of maps. These DRUs (many of which have already been mapped) are of the order of 10–100 Ha in area and have been characterised in terms of their possible response to different land uses reflected in the structuring of soils in each unit. This was not a mechanical operation. To begin with, apparently homogeneous regions were selected and investigated in terms of soil, water and vegetative properties. The results of these investigations were then analysed and a final decision made on the DRU boundaries. This was repeated for the whole of Crete until the island was capable of definition in terms of DRUs.

For each DRU, socio-economic impact will affect the natural environment in a defined way thus affecting economic productivity which feeds back into the model to alter its future evolution. As before, calibration then continues until predicted results equate to real data. The model is now ready to be used as a decision tool, in the way outlined in Chapter 5 – that is, by making interventions in year 1 and calculating the probability of certain environmental outcomes in year n through techniques such as those of risk analysis. The main point to emphasise is the need (as we see it) to include environmental factors directly in modelling activity. In saying this we do not intend to belittle or criticise other approaches to dealing with environmental regulation such as, for example, applying various forms of taxation on polluting activities. On the contrary the need for effective policy instruments is perennial. What we are saying, however, is that the long-term evolution of socio-economic systems can only be understood properly if they are linked organically to the natural systems of which they are a part.

6.5   THE MODEL AS A TRAINING METHODOLOGY

It is probably worth re-emphasising a more generic point about our methodology which relates to the more fundamental position we take about the scientific method outlined above. Traditionally, science's job is to tell about what is (reality) by means of experiment and validation rules. And that is fine provided that reality does not change over the time period under investigation. The problem is, however, that human systems evolve very fast indeed and so our conclusion is that the best we can achieve is a limited engagement with rapid change of complex systems.

It follows that the distinction between 'research' and 'training' is not the clear one as enshrined in the institutional structures of most academic bodies, but on the contrary is really part of the same knowledge-seeking process. The model is simply a means of achieving greater understanding. Furthermore, because the people most concerned with the system are actually participating in its functioning, it is very important that they themselves should also be directly involved. This is so not only because they are participants *per se* but also because their particular experiences and knowledge need to be mobilised as part of the research process itself.

What our computerised model does is to provide a means for all concerned agents to engage directly and in concert, in a process of collective research about their own system's evolution. In a sense the model acts as an integrating node and a language of discourse for a range of people and organisations who are separated by a wide variety of interests and perceptions, including perceptions about the nature of reality itself and how it may be understood. It is this interactive feature, rather than the sheer computing power of modern generations of computers, we should argue, that gives the approach we use a distinctiveness from older dynamical models of apparently similar kinds.

Ideally, however, it would be better if the models used were themselves generated by those directly concerned with managing the system in question – that is, the stakeholders. Traditionally simulation modelling as a tool in science and policy making has depended upon mainframe applications, which require extensive experience in the use of large computers and compilers such as FORTRAN or C. Even in the case of simulation languages, such as DYNAMO, developments have been limited to what is known as 'Batch Mode', which means that the simulation is done off-line. Consequently the modelling activity is often left to the 'system expert' who is assigned the task of translating a problem, as it has been formulated by a group of stakeholders, into a dynamic simulation. This inevitably creates a 'perception gap' between the group and the modeller's interpretation of their collective understanding, hence limiting the model's usefulness.

However, the situation has changed dramatically in the past few years with the development of new interactive modelling tools such as the VENSIM environment described in Appendix II. The principal advantage of VENSIM is the friendliness of the system for developing and running dynamic models. The ease of modelling resides in the interaction between the user and the different alternatives of output representation such as diagrams, graphs and tables. The model can be constructed and debugged in a fraction of the time it would take to develop an analogous model using traditional programming languages such as FORTRAN, or even simulation languages like DYNAMO. Once the model is constructed, the simulation run can be stopped and examined at any moment, and easily modified. In this way the user can quickly complete the tasks of debugging and calibrating the model and spend more time learning from the modelling exercise. He can also bring his own experience and knowledge more directly to bear on the problem, and at the same time is not so dependent on an outside 'expert'.

6.6   THE EQUATIONS

Most of the equations which we have used for our model have an exponential form known as a random utility function. There are at least two reasons for this. One is that the use of exponential equations permits the 'switching on' of key variables at appropriate temporal points in the calibration process. For example, an equation of the form:[12]

$$A_{ij}^l = exp\left(-\rho \times \left(p_i^l + ts^l \times d_{ij}\right)\right) \qquad (6.1)$$

allows the independent variables to vary their temporal influence on the dependent variable simply because the relationship is an additive one, and hence the parameters can be set equal to zero when necessary. If the equation were 'multiplicative' this would not be possible. From the standpoint of policy intervention this is a very useful property. The second reason is that the use of an exponential functional form allows us to employ 'rationality parameters' which, as we discuss below, therefore permits the simulation of diverse behaviour on the part of economic agents. It means also that the idea of microeconomic behaviour influencing macroeconomic outcomes is directly built into the model.

On the related question of calibration, the most important distinction to be made here is that of substantive as opposed to intermediary variables. The former represent variables for which actual data are available and which can hence be inserted directly into the model at various stages, particularly in defining the initial conditions for the simulation model. In the case of the Crete model the substantive variables for which data were obtained included the rural and urban population of Crete (NOS, 1984), employment in each of the three economic sectors in the model (Chania Statistical Office, 1992; Blue Plan, 1992), the available area in each region for each economic activity (Kolodny, 1974; Allbaugh, 1953), and values for labour productivity (Chania Statistical Office, 1992).

Intermediary variables on the other hand represent really the model's internal logic and should not be thought of (at least initially) as empirical quantities. For example, running an early version of the Crete model over the 1971–81 period in time steps of 52 per year (i.e. weekly time steps) produces an average price/unit cost ratio for agricultural production in zone 2 (urban) of approximately 100:1 in 1975. Within the model's operations this produces the appropriate incentive signals but clearly it does not equate to underlying realities of the economic system itself. On the other hand it is consistent with the temporal behaviour of the substantive variables.

Where counterintuitive results of this kind are obtained, the intermediary variables in question should now become the focus for more detailed analysis involving re-alignment of the model's parameters. It may be, for example, that certain parametric changes will re-configure the intermediary variables in question without doing violence to the model itself, in which case improved understanding of the Cretan economy will result. A second approach might be to expand the number of sectors (and/or zones), provided data are available, to see if a richer modelling scheme provides more realistic intermediate quantities. In this way (and others) the model becomes a focus for more detailed research and exploration about the underlying realities of the Crete economy and its development.

In fact since we are dealing explicitly with the *long-term* evolution of the economic system the importance of markets and prices becomes much less than it would be if we were analysing *short-term* economic behaviour. The strategic behaviour of the actors involved has little to do with how markets behave for this or that commodity, but on the contrary is determined fundamentally by expectations about long-term trends. As we have outlined in Chapter 4, such expectations are heuristic in nature and will depend upon a variety of cultural, social, political, economic and environmental factors, whose overall impact will vary across time and space (see also Appendix I).

A related point concerns the use of weekly time steps in the Crete model. This procedure was chosen simply because it appeared to allow the model to function without 'crashing'. There is nothing inherently magical about this procedure. A sequence of 52 time steps becomes part of the model's mathematical logic, but this does not mean necessarily that economic behaviour, for example, is based on 'weekly' decisions. All it does mean is that at a broad level the model's specification is not inconsistent with observed reality. When suitably calibrated it will run, and hence allow further research to proceed. If such research suggests that a rather different set of time steps is more appropriate, then the model may be altered to accommodate this.

6.7 SYSTEM DYNAMICS

A point which perhaps ought also to be stressed at this stage concerns the relationship of our approach to that of the better-known System Dynamics, of Forrester (and Meadows).[13] When these models were first suggested around the early 1970s they were received with considerable interest but subjected also to considerable criticism. For example, one complaint was that the attempt to model the world on a grand scale inevitably brought with it the need to make rather crude assumptions about parametric structures, for example, that existing dispositions of nationhood and political power would not change, or that new technologies would not radically transform consumption possibilities for the world as a whole. Another criticism was that such modelling represented a crude attempt to abstract from issues of social and economic power and to see the world in mechanistic terms.

Finally there were a range of more fundamental methodological criticisms relating to the overall structure and use of Forrester-type computer models. These concerned factors like the division of the aggregate model into 'submodels' dealing with pollution, capital, energy, agriculture and so on, and their reintegration into the main model. One group performed a series of empirical tests on the Forrester model showing how sensitive its predictions were to slight variations in its initial specifications. For example, it was shown that running the model backwards in time produced a world population of some two billion in 1880, a level more than four times the actual value and one that was not reached in practice until the late 1970s.[14]

In retrospect at least some of this criticism was probably a little unfair. Although there were clearly problems with the system dynamics approach, many of these were recognised by their exponents who saw systems modelling at a global level as an antidote to national bias and as a contribution to the sustainable development of a world that was becoming increasingly globalised. They did not argue that it was a perfect contribution. Merely that it was worthwhile pursuing for a variety of sensible reasons. For example, the charge that global modelling reduces the arena for social choice and moral comment is clearly not sustainable. On the contrary a perfectly good case can be made for precisely the opposite view. There is now so much information available to decision makers in modern economic systems that most decision makers find it increasingly difficult to separate out what is fact from what is actually *claimed* to be fact on the basis of ideological values and/or vested interests. What the construction and use of a model does is essentially to help clarify what can be accepted by all stakeholders as *fact*, so as to highlight essential differences of interest and value. In our view it is precisely the confusion between these two spheres that produces so much confusion, confusion that is then often used by unscrupulous agencies to pursue particularistic ends unconstrained by social and moral accountability.

For these and other reasons, therefore, we take the view that the use of models as an aid to policy choice and implementation is certainly to be encouraged. Indeed the Forrester/Meadows approach was a useful contribution to the field and a welcome antidote to the unduly static macroeconomic models that have continued to dominate this genre over the past twenty or so years. There is, however, an important difference between the Forrester/Meadows approach and our own and that is that while the former seeks to build a descriptive dynamic model of a system, that is calibrated so that it will reproduce some observed changes, our own model sets out to try to generate the system structure on the basis of processes occurring at a lower level. In other words, System Dynamics has a single analytical level, while our approach has two.

For example, in the case of a regional model, System Dynamics would take the units as given – cities, towns, rural areas, and so on – and simply model the interactions between them, and the changes that result as the model runs. The parameters would be point specific, and would reflect the different functions at each point. Our approach, however, tries to consider the multiple human decision makers underlying the model, and to examine the different criteria for their behaviour. The behavioural parameters that are used are supposed to be the same throughout the system, *as it has been calibrated*, but in scenario forecasts may well be changed, as we have seen.

Thus the spatial structure that exists is generated by the interactions, the processes that are involved in the system and in particular the non-linearities of these. Concentrations of economic activity are the result of positive feedbacks, where some initial nuclei are reinforced by increasing returns for location of activities in specific regions. The spatial structure of the system is therefore not taken as being fixed necessarily, but instead as being the result of an ongoing evolutionary process, which could change and restructure as other non-linearities became important, or if external conditions change.

Another way of making the same point is to emphasise the essential interlinkages and feedbacks between microeconomic agents and macroeconomic impacts which our model attempts to capture. The System Dynamics of the Forrester/Meadows approach does not permit the perceptions (and therefore the actions) of micro agents to influence events. These are simply viewed as characteristics of the system encapsulated as system parameters. Conversely the approach of this book explicitly introduces behaviour through the use of 'attractivities' which change continuously as the system evolves. These attractivities are the mechanism by which small differences in productivity can be amplified through self-reinforcing processes (e.g. higher profits generating new job opportunities, attracting labour which improves productivity), leading eventually to a spatial re-structuring of the system as a whole.

As mentioned briefly above, the actual mechanism used is the use of 'rationality parameters', such as ρ and λ in equations (AI.2) and (AI.22) respectively shown in Appendix I. For example, equation (AI.22) shows how populations move amongst regions according to perceptions of advantage and in this case the relevant residential attractivity parameter is λ . This effectively reflects the behavioural homogeneity of the migrating population. Where all individual households behave exactly the same, then $\lambda = 1$. On the other hand, where there are differences in behaviour then $0 < \lambda < 1$, and the greater the behavioural differences the smaller the (positive) value of the parameter. Calibration proceeds by choosing the parametric value that best fits the available data.[15]

Of course, choice of this parameter does not mean that populations will always continue to exhibit the same degree of behavioural heterogeneity in future periods. Circumstances may well change and these will then be reflected in the model's parametric structure. The point is, however, that by including the notion of behavioural differences on the part of actors, the model explicitly recognises the role of *micro* behaviour as affecting, and at the same time being affected by, *macro* outcomes. Evolutionary and systemic complexity is built directly into the model's implicit logic, which in turn is then reflected in its use as a generator of future planning and policy scenarios.

6.8   POLICY AND POLICY ANALYSIS

It remains for us finally to explore briefly what our approach has to contribute to theory and practice in the formulation, implementation and evaluation of public policy. It will be recalled that we opened Chapter 1 with the aim of exploring how the use of non-linear models can improve the integrated management of social and natural systems with particular reference to Third World countries. Of course this brings us immediately into the realm of policy, policy analysis and policy research, fields that have been growing in interest over recent years and which may well be ready for a fresh approach.

The theory of public policy is not new, of course. It goes back certainly to the 1950s and the era of the 'think tanks' such as the Rand Corporation and the Brookings Institution in the USA, and very probably to pre-war writing. Kean argues, however, that since that time 'much of the literature in policy science ... [has] ... had a strong linearity in its conceptual framework'.[16] At least this has certainly been true in the UK and the USA. He argues that traditional theories of public policy assume a rationalist mode which concentrates almost exclusively on the *formulation* of policy (policy rhetoric) and within which individual groups of economic actors have no autonomous role beyond that of being operational 'agents of policy'.

In a detailed survey he divides this literature into three distinctive types (decision theory, organisation theory and political analysis) each of which, however, are essentially rational in nature – in so far as they stress generalised means/ends interactions that can be applied to all circumstances. Policies are drawn up (sometimes on the basis of a standard calculus like that of social cost/benefit analysis), and if they do not achieve what they are intended to achieve, this is often held not to be a problem of the policy-making process itself but rather one of political or managerial failure in implementing policies. Put another way, much of the emphasis in the standard literature concentrates very much upon generalised statements about the policy-making process, but tends then to be relatively weak on following through what actually happens in practice and then using this knowledge to inform theory. It is Kean's position that all too often what actually happens in practice is that policy outcomes bear very little relationship to policy decisions. The *rhetoric* of policy is one thing. Its *result* is quite another. Indeed there are often powerful ideological reasons why policy makers are often reluctant to face the consequences of their actions.

Criticism of this (mechanistic) position is not new, of course. The classic article by Lindblom, in which he argues that the most effective type of policy procedures should avoid *ex ante* means/ends formulae, was originally published in 1959. Since then a small band of iconoclasts such as Clay and Schaffer (eds) (1984) and Thomas and Grindle (1990), for example, have continued to argue similar positions by emphasising the importance of institutional power politics and the importance for the policy implementer of preserving 'room for manoeuvre'. And we have already noted in Chapter 1 Ostrom's detailed evidence on organisational variability. On the policy evaluation side, political scientists such as Freeman (1985) and Rose (1991), have begun to favour a more inductive approach based upon comparative case studies of specific sectors and countries which admit of only broad policy trends. Nevertheless, Kean argues, it is probably not unfair to conclude that much of the prevailing wisdom in the 'policy sciences' is mechanistic in the sense defined above.

A similar view is taken by Röling in a brief review of the literature on communications strategies for natural resource management (NRM). Röling's position is that what is now needed is what he calls *platform processes* designed to improve participation in NRM and associated policy activity, citing a range of methodologies including applications of 'soft systems' (Checkland, 1981; Checkland and Scholes, 1990), 'participatory technology development' (Jiggins and de Zeeuw, 1992), 'farming field schools' (van de Fliert, 1993) and 'participatory rural appraisal' (Chambers, 1994).

It is on this point that we would argue the possibilities inherent in our approach. The models outlined in Chapters 4 and 5 are designed as tools to enfranchise the stakeholders (or their representatives) in the socio-economic systems under analysis. Although they appear to be rather complex, they have been presented this way mainly to demonstrate the logic underlying their essential properties. Properly used, however, they have the potential, we believe, to 'democratise' both the formulation and implementation of public (and indeed private) policy in fundamental senses. Instead of policy activity being a 'top down', mechanistic endeavour attempting somehow to emulate the exactitude of some of our natural sciences, it accepts the evolutionary and self-organising realities of economic systems and tries to come to terms with this fact. The models are to be used as 'languages of discourse' and as 'promoters of informed discussion and debate' amongst all relevant political and professional interests.

Policy formulation, implementation and evaluation then proceed in ways that allow much more participation than has been traditionally the case in many countries. 'Top down' and 'bottom up' become integrated in a common search for policy interventions that genuinely promote the welfare of all citizens independent of ruling ideologies and vested interests, and with the confidence that the system being acted upon is the real system and not some mechanical ideal left over from the nineteenth century.

6.9   CONCLUSIONS

The problem of how to understand the evolutionary behaviour of economic systems is only now being fully recognised, we would argue, and this is probably because the reality of change, its pace and its potentially destructive consequences are beginning to impinge much more directly on many more people and organisations for the first time in recorded history. In a very real sense the earth is becoming a 'global village' in which events in any part have irreversible consequences in all other parts. Under these circumstances it is no longer desirable, we believe, to attempt to understand its behaviour through the use of models derived from traditional approaches based upon single disciplines such as economics, for example. To do so is simply inefficient in every sense of the word.

We began this book by pointing out that conventional ways of thinking about socio-economic systems have been influenced to a great extent by an underlying assumption that they behave like physical systems. This being so, the models that are used to explore their behaviour are not only mechanistic in content (they seek general and deterministic solutions that are universally applicable across time and space), but they tend also to build up barriers between the many disciplines that each have a role to play in providing a better understanding of how such systems really function. We argued that while this is inappropriate generally, it is especially so when we are considering the sustainable development of Third World systems. Indeed it is doubtful whether the notion of sustainability can ever be unambiguously defined in relation to complex systems that are evolving as rapidly as is evident in many such countries today. Instead there is a need for perhaps less ambitious programmes where the fact of our partial incertitude is explicitly recognised and where policy analysis is similarly informed.

In this book we have put forward a broad dynamical modelling schema which we believe may be a useful first step towards integrating environmental and technological considerations into development policy. The model has been applied to Senegal and to the island economy of Crete as part of an ongoing research programme which has both methodological as well as substantive objectives. It is planned to produce a series of empirically based papers on this theme over the next few years. Although much remains to be done, it is our argument that this (interdisciplinary) approach deserves further consideration in the fight to preserve our environment from the potentially irreversible and damaging consequences of uncontrolled economic development.

NOTES

1   As far as we know there is no *one* set of definitions that is universally accepted regarding 'knowledge' and its correlate, 'information', though see Davies (ed.) (1994) for a recent volume dealing with development-related issues. Our own way of thinking about both concepts is to think of them both systemically but to treat the latter, information, as a more general entropic notion. Thus there is always a considerable amount of 'information' available to the actors in any economic system (indeed often far too much), but it only becomes 'knowledge' when it is seen to be useful for actual behaviour. See also Clark (1992) and Clark and Juma (1992).

2   See, for example, Barnes (1982) who cites Gruber and Marquis (eds) (1969) as one of the earliest attempts to argue the case for an interactive view of relations between science and production. This point is noted in Hicks (1995). See also Kline (1985).

3   See Rosen (1974), p. 245.

4   Ibid., p. 246.

5   Edge (1988), p. 1. Emphasis is in the original text.

6   See also Clark (1992).

7   Actually this perspective depends on a rather older tradition in the sociology of knowledge deriving from Toulmin, Polanyi, Kuhn and others which stresses the socially constructed nature of *all* knowledge. See, for example, Collins (1992).

8   Gass and Biggs (1993), p. 4.

9   See, for example, Chambers (1994) and Röling (1994). Röling is interesting because he

summarises and references a growing literature on participatory methods for natural resource management more generally, including those relevant to the industrialised countries. He argues that the complexity of modern systems is such that new types of professional persons have become much in demand to orchestrate system intervention.

10 Stirling (1994) has recently suggested a similar approach in relation to the planning of an appropriate mix of energy projects. His starting point is to build 'diversity' directly into the calculation using an index derived from formal information theory. In this way, he argues, it is possible to take our relative ignorance of future states of nature into account and to separate points of political dispute more easily from those of objective analysis.

11 There is a close correspondence between the techniques being developed here and those of a Dutch group at the Research Institute for Knowledge Systems (RIKS). The RIKS team use what they describe as a 'cellular automata' technique, to distribute global data over smaller units of space. They have done this in a number of planning contexts including especially that of island economies in the Caribbean. See, for example, Engelen et al. (1993) and White and Engelen (1993).

12 i.e. equation (AI.1) in Appendix I.

13 See Forrester (1971) and Meadows et al. (1972) for an exposition of the original World models. See also Cole et al. (eds) (1973) and Encel et al. (1975) for a detailed critique of this genre.

14 See article by Cole and Curnow, in Cole et al. (eds) (1973), pp. 108–34.

15 For a detailed discussion on the use of rationality parameters, see Allen and Sanglier (1981) and Allen and McGlade (1986).

16 See Kean (1994), p. 20.

Appendix I An Exploration of Complex Economic Systems Modelling for Strategic Planning

AI.1 INTRODUCTION

A major issue in contemporary development planning is how to ensure sustained and balanced development in economic systems. An important part of the problem lies in the evolutionary complexity and self-organisation of such systems where the interactive behaviour of relevant actors is very difficult to predict with any realism. A related difficulty concerns how we define and conceptualise the system under investigation. Conventional approaches tend generally to a high degree of abstraction from reality. This often means that vital interrelationships are ignored which can have a notable effect on overall system management.

This research, which explores the complexity of economic systems for strategic planning, had its origins in the 1970s with the building of a series of regional demographic models, initially for Belgium and later for the USA and other countries. However, its aim in recent years has been to provide an integrated framework and decision tool within which the complex and multiple consequences of development planning and policy can be examined in as complete a way as possible. It has been applied to a number of countries, including some which are facing considerable problems of natural resource management, and there have been consistent improvements made to its scope and accuracy as a result.

This appendix presents an integrated software framework in which an improvement on the core model has been made based on dynamic interregional input–output flows. Feedback loops of capital investment and the attractiveness of investment have been added into the mathematical simulation model, in our view improving its accuracy and verisimilitude. Together with some other improvements on demand, costs, profit, import, export and employment, we believe that this makes the core model closer to the real world. Section AI.2 provides an introduction to the modelling framework linking population, economic activities and the ecosystem. Section AI.3 describes in detail the core simulation model of economic systems, while Section AI.4 gives a specific example of the Senegal model as a strategic planning tool for exploring different development scenarios.

AI.2 MODELLING FRAMEWORK

The modelling framework consists of several spatial and dynamic submodels, such as a population submodel, a natural resource submodel and an economic submodel (see Figure AI.1), in which the demographic, economic and environment variables which link each other are presented. The central elements are migration, investment and land/water use which experience strategic change in the long term.

Figure AI.1 Basic modelling framework

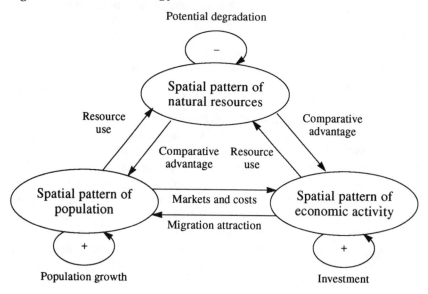

From the view of spatial structure, the demographic, economic and environment variables in the modelling framework are disaggregated into those for different regions and sectors. The spatial structure that exists is generated by the interactions among regions and sectors which in turn strengthen non-linearities and feedback features. In this way the spatial structure of the system is not fixed , but instead is the result of an ongoing evolutionary process, which could change and restructure as other non-linearities become important or if external conditions change – for example, the change of spatial dimensionality to the space or water supply available for any given economic activity and residence of the population. Most importantly, it introduces three behaviours through the use of an 'attractivity' term for demand, migration and investment.

These attractivities are the mechanism by which small differences in price, reward and productivity can be amplified through self-reinforcing processes leading eventually to a spatial re-structuring of the system as a whole. Economic incentives and investment attractivities create opportunities for employment, increasing vacancies and raising labour productivity, bringing about increases in jobs and wages. The improved income-earning opportunities then alter relative economic conditions among the regions and increase the attractivity of other regions to the workforce which in turn alters relative investment behaviour in each sector. Thus from the standpoint of any particular region there may be incentives favouring migration from other regions and possibly further investment in that region. On the other hand, there will be further growth of population and potential degradation of the environment, particularly as a result of greater use of land, water and fuel. Potential degradation could then lead to a loss of comparative advantages in economic activity and residence. Such a combination of positive and negative feedback loops may turn the balance of advantage in different directions, and change spatial patterns of economic activity and population migration.

One of the notable characteristics of the modelling framework is that the economic model in it is based on interregional input–output analysis. Most of the economic variables in the causal-loop diagram (see Figure AI.2), such as demand and supply, import and export, accumulation and consumption, depreciation, costs, wages and profits, link directly with an interregional input–output system which differs from the conventional one in that it is evolutionary. Flows of inputs from different sectors and regions per unit of time are converted by a productive sector and a distributive process into flows of outputs to different sectors and regions. In this complex converting process, the unit prices of goods and services for different sectors and regions vary over time according to differences between demands and supplies in each of them, in turn bringing about changes in costs, profits, investments and the spatial economic structure. In this way there is a constant tendency to instability mediated by market mechanisms. The interregional input–output table establishes a relationship between the whole economy and its regional/sectorial and local decision-making components. In other words it establishes a relationship between 'macro' economic behaviour and 'micro' economic structure.

The modelling framework includes also an interactive software package to run the simulation model. An intervention can be made during the simulation by selecting the appropriate menu, different types of policies or decisions and the factors which are directly affected. The parameters affected by the intervention can then be modified. The time-series charts, the map display of the changing value and the summary of the numerical data can be made as the model is used. In addition, different development scenarios can be printed and stored. In this way, it is very simple for decision makers, planners and policy analysts to anticipate how an economic system may respond to a possible action or policy.

Figure AI.2 Basic causal feedback

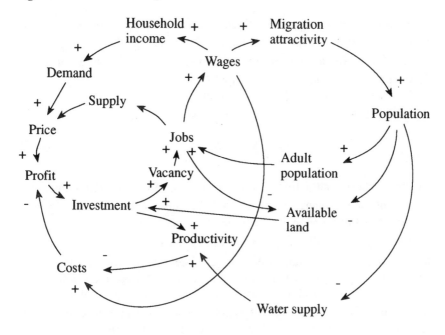

AI.3 THE CORE SIMULATION MODEL

AI.3.1 Demand and Supply

Suppose the economic systems under consideration are split into n regions $(1, 2, 3 ...i, j ...n)$ and m sectors $(1, 2, 3, ...l, ...m)$. The core model describes the economic activities on the level of these sectors and regions. For every sector and every region, there is a similar set of variables in it.

It is useful to describe the model in detail by starting off with the notion of 'attractivity' which is used to define conditions under which economic agents (for example, consumers, investors and migrators) will be induced to alter their behaviour in specific ways. Ask the question: what factors will influence the demand behaviour of consumers in region j with respect to purchases of good l from all regions $i = 1, 2, 3, ...n$? We then define the attractivity of goods and services produced in i and abroad from the standpoint of consumers in j as:

$$A_{ij}^l = exp\left(-\rho \times \left(p_i^l + ts^l \times d_{ij}\right)\right) \qquad (AI.1)$$

$$exA_j^l = exp\left(-\rho \times WP_j^l\right) \qquad (AI.2)$$

where ρ represents a response rationality parameter, $P_i^l =$ price of sector l in region i, $ts^l \times d_{ij} =$ transport costs for a unit of l between i and j, $WP_j^l =$ world price of l including transport costs, exA_j^l is the attractivity of goods produced from abroad for the consumer j.

In order to find the relative attractivity, we must now sum over all the potential sources of goods l for the consumer j, to give:

$$SA_j^l = \sum_i A_{ij}^l + exA_j^l \qquad (AI.3)$$

so that relative attractivity is given by A_{ij}^l / SA_j^l and determines the proportion of the interregional demand for goods l that falls on region i, where $SA_j^l =$ total economic attractivity of goods l for the consumer j.

Partial demand PD_{ij}^l for goods l falling on region i and generated by another region j (including i) is then calculated as the sum of three terms. The first term is the final consumption demand falling on i which is a product of proportional function Φ and wealth WH_j in region j. The second term is the investment demand falling on i which is a product of proportional function Ψ and I_j in region j. The third term is the intersectorial demand falling on i from j.

$$PD_{ij}^l = \left| \frac{\Phi^l}{\sum_k \Phi^k} \times Wh_j + \frac{\Psi^l}{\sum_k \Psi^k} \times I_j + SD_j^l \times \left(P_i^l + ts^l x d_{ij}\right) \right| \times \frac{A_{ij}^l}{SA_j^l} \qquad (AI.4)$$

Intersectorial demand in j is given by:

$$SD_j^l = \sum_k X_{kl} \times J_j^k \times Py_j^k \qquad (AI.5)$$

X_{kl} is the element of an *mxm* input–output matrix X defined as the intersectorial demand for a lower-cost product l in order to produce a unit k of higher quality, $J_j^k=$ employment for sector k in region j and $Py_j^k=$ productivity for sector k in region j which is described by the following expression:

$$\frac{\partial Py_j^l}{\partial t} = \left(1+\omega^1 \times I_j^l\right) \times \left(1-\omega^2 \times \frac{space^l \times J_j^l}{Aa_j^l}\right) \times \left(1-\omega^3 \times \frac{WD_j^l}{WS_j^l}\right) \times Py_j^l \quad (AI.6)$$

where $\omega^1, \omega^2, \omega^3$ are respectively the coefficients of investment, land use and water supply contributing to productivity of sector l and region j, $I_j^l=$ available investment for sector l in region j, $Aa_j^l=$ the total area available for sector l in region j, $space^l =$ space requirement per job for sector l, $\dfrac{space^l \times J_j^l}{Aa_j^l}$ is a proportion of land use for sector l in region j, $WD_j^l=$ the annual water demand and $WS_j^l=$ the annual water supply for sector l in region j.

Total demand falling on sector l and region i will then consist of partial demands falling on i from all region j and external demand from overseas (export):

$$D_i^l = Ext_i^l + \sum_j PD_{ij}^l \qquad (AI.7)$$

where $Ext_i^l=$ export or demand from abroad in region i for goods l.

We are now in a position to compare total demand falling on i (in sector l) with total supply of goods l in i. This is given by:

$$S_j^l = J_i^l \times P_i^l \times Py_i^l \qquad (AI.8)$$

It is now possible to model the change in economic activity which will result from any disequilibrium between supply and demand in terms of a rate of desired expansion and a rate of price change:

$$\frac{\partial P_i^l}{\partial t} = \eta^l \times P_i^l \left(\frac{D_i^l}{S_i^l}-1\right) \qquad (AI.9)$$

Where η^l= a rate per year of price change comparing supply and demand.

AI.3.2 Costs, Profit and Income

The cost per unit of goods from sector l in region i is calculated as the sum of three terms:

$$C_i^l = \sum_k \sum_j x_{lk} \times \left(P_j^k + ts^k \times d_{ij}\right) \times \frac{A_{ji}^k}{SA_i^k} + \frac{W_i^l + Rt_i^l + De_i^l}{Py_i^l} + \sum_k x_{lk} \times WP_i^k \times \frac{exA_i^k}{SA_i^k} \quad \text{(AI.10)}$$

where W_i^l= wages paid for sector l and region i, Rt_i^l= rent costs per job for sector l and region i, De_i^l= depreciation for sector l and region i. The first term is an expression of the unit production costs involved in the necessary base products k from all regions j. The second term is an expression of unit costs of wages, rent and depreciation in sector l and zone i. The third term is unit production costs of foreign exchange for the necessary base product k.

Profit is then obtained by subtracting total costs from total revenue:

$$Pf_i^l = \left(P_i^l - C_i^l\right) \times J_i^l \times Py_i^l \quad \text{(AI.11)}$$

Incomes are of two kinds, wages and rents for each of the zones which are calculated as a function of total wages earned by the labour force, plus the earnings obtained from renting space to each of the economic sectors in that region. That is, total disposable income in any zone is given by:

$$Wh_i = \sum_l J_i^l \times \left(W_i^l + Rt_i^l\right) \quad \text{(AI.12)}$$

where wages are given by:

$$\frac{\partial W_i^l}{\partial t} = \gamma^l \times W_i^l \times \left(\frac{V_i^l}{J_i^l}\theta^l\right) \quad \text{(AI.13)}$$

where V_i^l= the vacancies for sector l in region i, γ = a change rate per year proportionally to itself and the excess of vacancies to jobs, θ = parameter of sensitivity of the wages to the job market.

Wages then determine regional income as described above, thus feeding back into the model and allowing it to continue to run. The end result is that the model generates continuous temporal data on economic output, jobs, land use and population.

AI.3.3 Attractiveness of Investment

We define and compute the attractivity of investment by sector and region according to profit as well as the limitation of land, i.e. available land. Of course, many more factors can be added into the attractivity but only two factors are considered here. The greater is the occupation of land or the smaller is the amount of available land, the lower is the attractivity of investment. At the same time the greater the expectation of profits, the greater is the attractivity of investment. The sectorial and regional attractivity of investment may then be described as follows:

$$IA_i^l = exp\left(\mu^1 \times \left(1 - \frac{space^l \times J_i^l}{Aa_i^l} \right) + \mu^2 \times \left(1 - \frac{P_i^l - C_i^l}{P_i^l} \right) \right) \qquad (AI.14)$$

where $1 - \frac{space^l \times J_i^l}{Aa_i^l}$ is a proportion of available land for sector l in region i, $1 - \frac{P_i^l - C_i^l}{P_i^l}$ is relative unit profit for sector l in region i, μ^1, μ^2 are the parameters of importance related to investment which weigh up profit against land.

In order to find the relative attractivity of investment, we must now sum over all the potential attraction, to give:

$$IA_i = \sum_l IA_i^l \qquad (AI.15)$$

$$IA = \sum_i \sum_l IA_i^l \qquad (AI.16)$$

so that relative attractivity of national investment is given by IA_i^l / IA, and relative attractivity of regional investment is given by IA_i^l / IA_i. Furthermore, we have investment for sector l and region i:

$$I_i^l = I \times \frac{IA_i^l}{IA} + I_i \times \frac{IA_i^l}{IA_i} \qquad (AI.17)$$

where I = total available national investment for all sectors and regions, and I_i = total available regional investment for all sectors in that region.

Capital accumulation is then obtained by:

$$\frac{\partial Ca_i^l}{\partial t} = I_i^l - De_i^l \qquad (AI.18)$$

AI.3.4 Vacancies and Migrations

In the model there is an important question regarding how much profit creates how many vacancies, and also one about how many vacancies cause how much migration between regions? The model calculates the number of new jobs in each region according to how well its sectors are generating profits per unit of output and how successful they are in attracting investment from other regions. At this stage, we are able to generate an expansion or contraction of the vacancies that could potentially be filled. When profit is positive, investment will increase, so vacancies will grow. When profit is negative, investment will fall, so vacancies will decline. The modified equation relates changes in vacancies as a function of relative investment and past trends in the labour market. The equations should be distinguished from different cases of profit and vacancy.

When profits are positive and vacancies are also positive the equations of jobs and vacancies are given by:

$$\frac{\partial J_i^l}{\partial t} = \sigma^l \times V_i^l \times \frac{Ue_i}{\sum_k J_i^k} \quad \text{and} \quad \frac{\partial V_i^l}{\partial t} = \frac{I_i^l}{\Gamma(Py_i^l)} - \sigma^l \times V_i^l \times \frac{Ue_i}{\sum_k J_i^k} \qquad \text{(AI.19)}$$

When profits are positive and vacancies are negative, a wise decision maker will stop dismissing employees. Conversely when profits are negative and vacancies are positive the opposite will be the case and so the equations are:

$$\frac{\partial J_i^l}{\partial t} = 0 \quad \text{and} \quad \frac{\partial V_i^l}{\partial t} = \frac{I_i^l}{\Gamma(Py_i^l)} \qquad \text{(AI.20)}$$

When both profits and vacancies are negative then the equation is:

$$\frac{\partial J_i^l}{\partial t} = \alpha^l \times V_i^l \quad \text{and} \quad \frac{\partial V_i^l}{\partial t} = \frac{I_i^l}{\Gamma(Py_i^l)} - \alpha^l \times V_i^l \qquad \text{(AI.21)}$$

where $\sigma, \alpha =$ the change rate per year of vacancy, $Ue_i =$ the level of unemployment, $\frac{Ue_i}{\sum_k J_i^k}$ is the proportion of unemployed to employed producing the pressure on the labour market. $\Gamma(Py_i^l) =$ the capital per job as a function of productivity for sector l in region i.

Closure of the model occurs by means of changes to the overall unemployed population in any region, which takes place as a result of in and out migration and its impact on vacancies. The model then calculates a term 'residential attractivity', which reflects the relative attractiveness of each region to potential migrants from other regions. This is calculated as a function of the average wages earned in a region relative to the average wages earned in all regions. Of course, the actual problem of migration can be quite complicated and involve many factors, but it is not difficult to add these into the equations.

$$R_i = exp\left(\lambda_i \times \frac{\sum_l W_i^l \times J_i^l}{\sum_l J_i^l} \right) \qquad (AI.22)$$

Where λ_i represents a response rationality parameter, $\dfrac{\sum_l W_i^l \times J_i^l}{\sum_l J_i^l}$ = the average wages in region i, and the relative residential attractivity is $R_i / \sum_i R_i$.

Finally the migration equation is given by:

$$\frac{dPop_i}{dt} = b_i \times Pop_i - m_i \times Pop_i + M + \Sigma_j Pop_j \times \frac{\Sigma R_{ij}}{\Sigma_j' R_{j\,i}'} \qquad (AI.23)$$

where b_i = birth rate; m_i = death rate; Pop_j = population at j; Pop_i = population at i; R_{ij} = attractivity of i when viewed from j and M = mobility parameter.

AI.4 APPLICATION: STRATEGIC PLANNING FOR SENEGAL

The modelling framework has been used to explore policies for the regional development of Senegal. The Senegal model has been built according to the improved core simulation model mentioned above (see Section AI.3) describing economic activities in Senegal at the level of six sectors in ten regions, as well as population and environment. The six sectors are fishing, extensive agriculture, intensive agriculture, industry, public service and an 'other tertiary' sector. It has been calibrated using census and economic data from Senegal to generate the temporal evolution of the system for the period 1980–90. It has then been used to explore the economic, demographic and environment dynamics of the system to assess the consequences of future scenarios in the Dakar and St Louis regions for 1995 and 2000 (see Table AI.1), thus providing a tool for evaluating strategic planning and polices for Senegal. For example, Figure AI.3 and Figure AI.4 present separately the model results for the spatial dynamics of employment and output in Dakar and St Louis for the 1980–2000 period. The interesting outcome of this simulation is that it gives a notable comparison of changes in agriculture, industry and services for Dakar and St Louis which should be helpful in exploring policies for the regional development of Senegal.

Table AI.1   A simulation scenario of Senegal

Simulation variables	Measure unit	Year 1990	Year 1995	Year 2000
Population	k* person	7020.26	8083.91	9316.22
Dakar		1529.80	1860.54	2261.21
St Louis		706.24	797.18	899.76
Employment	k* person	2712.92	3313.15	3718.65
Dakar		423.18	565.43	585.79
Agriculture		41.71	41.80	41.80
Industry		112.67	199.98	200.00
Services		269.67	324.24	343.99
St Louis		305.77	354.17	400.86
Agriculture		178.13	193.50	216.25
Industry		31.41	42.05	49.76
Services		96.46	118.89	135.04
Output	m* CFA	2980438	4020050	4443518
Dakar		689645	993166	1050314
Agriculture		29321	31553	32150
Industry		393727	584528	613273
Services		302597	377085	404891
St Louis		306765	376517	423941
Agriculture		120156	149943	164080
Industry		68997	80298	96313
Services		117612	146276	163548
Productivity	ton/	8909	9595	9677
Dakar	k* person	15815	18505	18345
St Louis		7351	7649	7736
Income	m* CFA	1187837	1568567	1841212
Dakar		260899	390586	424793
St Louis		106968	134041	161193
Profit	m* CFA	806415	969577	968441
Dakar		179067	160578	169885
St Louis		90324	110667	112245
Investment	m* CFA	1080023	1309940	1347893
Dakar		232630	235678	247170
St Louis		118993	140648	145927

Figure AI.3 The changes of employment in Dakar and St Louis between 1980 and 2000

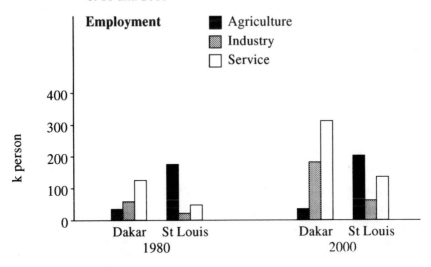

Figure AI.4 The changes of output in Dakar and St Louis between 1980 and 2000

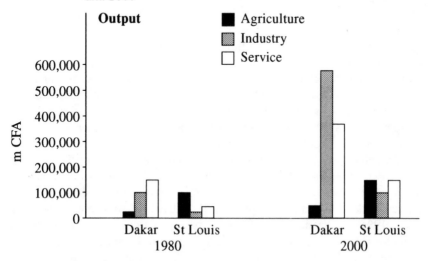

Appendix II   VENSIM: A Modelling Environment

AII.1   INTRODUCTION

System dynamic modelling has traditionally been considered a complicated task, requiring special training in the concepts of system dynamics and in programming in languages such as FORTRAN, BASIC, C, or PASCAL. It is factors like this which have often tended to restrict the usefulness of system dynamics in interdisciplinary applications, such as managing land degradation and desertification, in spite of the dynamic nature of these kinds of problems. Nevertheless it is widely acknowledged that there is a need for better decision-making tools for those who are not systems modellers or programmers but whose professional capacities could be enhanced in this way. Simulation environments such as STELLA and VENSIM, which run on computers with a WINDOWS capacity and which can be used to simulate systems which are subject to time-dependent processes with the purpose of improving thinking and learning, were originally inspired by Jay Forrester's (1968) theories of system dynamics. More recently STELLA, a modelling environment which runs on the Apple Macintosh, has been used in the development of spatial landscape models (Boumans and Sklar,1990; Costanza and Maxwell, 1991; Ring and Sklar 1989; Sklar and Costanza, 1991), in modelling the evolution of structure in Mediterranean soils (Perez-Trejo,1995), in the development of population ecology models (Wu and Vankat, 1992) and in assessing environmental impacts (Mitch, Cronk and Sykes, 1990).

VENSIM itself has been developed as a convenient tool for the analysis of the different modelling components that underlie water resource management. In particular it demonstrates a process-oriented approach to the understanding and management of desertification (Perez-Trejo and Saez, 1995). The notation of model representation, shown here in the different model stages, consists of flows regulated by state variables (rates of change) and constants (parameters) which act together to produce the dynamic in the stock or storage of a state variable (see Figure AII.1). In addition the environment has been developed by Perez-Trejo and Saez (1995) as a series of models of increasing complexity starting from a very simple example of an infiltration process and progressing to a model that reflects both the spatial and temporal aspects of water re-distribution in the soil/plant system as well as the evolution of structure in the landscape system as a whole. For those whose computer skills are at a rudimentary stage VENSIM has been designed so that no such skills are required, and indeed this can make the whole modelling exercise appear deceptively easy given the friendliness of its representation. Finally the system model is developed on the computer screen using explicit structural diagrams, graphics and tables which allow the user to evaluate the overall effects of the interrelations or processes that have been simulated.

In the following sections we introduce the principal concepts of the VENSIM modelling system, the assumptions which underlie the approach, and the advantages and limitations which must be taken into account in understanding the structure and results of the exercise as a whole. For purposes of illustration we have exemplified the technique using the case of population dynamics and that of a simple reservoir system which has water flowing into it and out of it. Further details may be seen with reference to Perez-Trejo and Saez (1995).

AII.2   THE MODELLING ENVIRONMENT

In using VENSIM, the user develops the model as a flow diagram from a 'tool kit' of modelling elements, such as state variables, flows and parameters, which can be selected with the mouse-driven pointer. A modelling element is selected from the 'tool-kit' by clicking on the mouse and positioning it in the VENSIM work-space. The different elements are then linked together to simulate the structural relationships assumed to exist among them. At this stage only a limited number of the possibilities of VENSIM are used, mainly those needed in the first stage of discovering the behaviour of the structural relationships and the formulation of the associated equations.

All models developed in VENSIM are composed of five object types which represent the components of the system. A brief description of the different modelling elements shown in Figure AII.1 may be helpful to acquaint the reader with the meaning of each of the symbols included in the tool-kit (Figures AII.3 and AII.4) and as a way of introducing some key concepts in systems thinking. The first is a *state variable* or *stock* representing accumulation (net inflows minus outflows) and is drawn in the tool-kit as a half-full box. The (double) flow-lines with black arrowheads represent the *movement of material* from or towards state variables.

Control of the flow between sinks, sources and state variables is exhibited by the double triangles representing control valves. The flow-lines are connected to clouds which indicate *external sinks or sources* of the open system. The circles in the diagram represent *constants, functions or non-state variables* which are linked to state variables, valves or other circles by thin-lined connection arrows. These connection arrows indicate a *functional relationship* between two system objects.

Figure AII.1 Modelling elements used to develop dynamic models in VENSIM

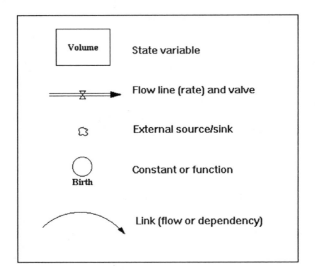

A state variable is defined by selecting the square from the tool-kit and placing it somewhere in the work-space (Figure AII.2). The user completes the structure of the model by selecting 'flow-lines', 'parameters' and 'links' to develop a graphical representation of the system.

The next element is an 'auxiliary variable', which is used either to set the input for a flow, or to set the value of a constant which is used elsewhere in the model. The arrow-shaped tool is the 'link'. It is used to represent the data paths between different elements in the system. The flow-line (rate) is the element which defines the way in which the variables in the system change. A flow-line can either connect two state variables, or simply flow into or out of a stock. The cloud symbol attached at the end of a flow-line represents the boundary of the system which is not simulated explicitly.

Figure AII.2   The VENSIM workspace

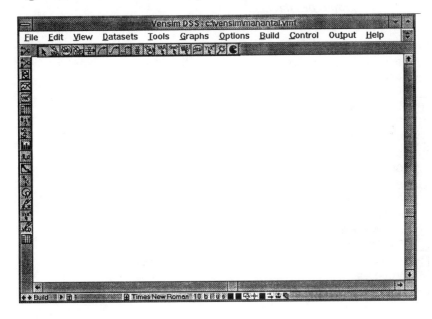

Figure AII.3   VENSIM tool-kit along the top margin

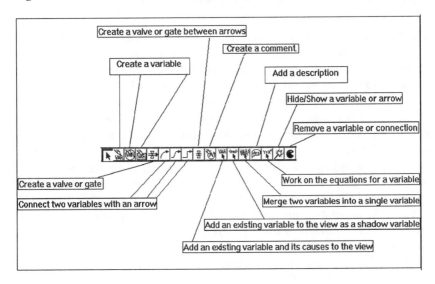

Figure AII.4 VENSIM buttons along the left margin to represent outputs as graphs or tables.

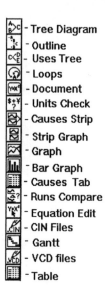

- Tree Diagram
- Outline
- Uses Tree
- Loops
- Document
- Units Check
- Causes Strip
- Strip Graph
- Graph
- Bar Graph
- Causes Tab
- Runs Compare
- Equation Edit
- CIN Files
- Gantt
- VCD files
- Table

AII.3   BUILDING A MODEL IN VENSIM

The first step in building a model in VENSIM is to develop a conceptual model of the system of interest. This is a very important phase of the exercise and it usually requires the input of more that one person and of people who have empirical knowledge of the system. The conceptual model consists of an explicit statement of the essential components of the system, of the processes which link these components, and of the factors which affect these processes. One of the most useful tools in developing such a conceptual model is the causal-loop diagram which can help the modeller in formalising a hypothesis about the way the system is actually structured. Several examples of causal-loop diagrams are presented in Perez-Trejo and Saez (1995).[1] The conceptual model then serves as a framework to develop a VENSIM simulation model but as it starts to take shape, and quickly produce results, modellers usually start to revise or improve their original conceptual model. This is not a negative aspect of the model-building exercise. On the contrary, it is probably where most learning takes place. It is this dialogue between the modellers and their collective understanding of a system coupled to the structured modelling tool which can help to advance the science beyond the disciplinary single-dimension approach.

Figure AII.5 The window for inputting equations of a state variable (VOLUME)

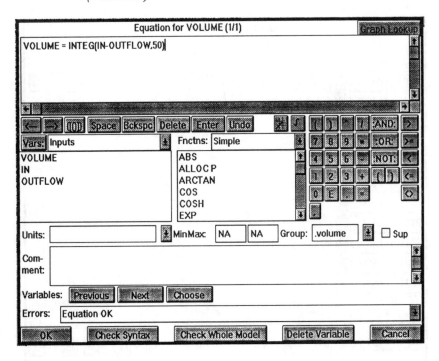

Having developed the conceptual model, the modeller then goes to the VENSIM system to begin building the associated simulation model. Figure AII.5 illustrates the way in which the equation for a state variable is built up by combining the required inputs displayed in the left-hand window in a mathematical equation which represents its dynamics over time. The numeric keys on the right-hand side of the display can be used to include numbers or logical operators in the equation. The box on the middle-top, labelled 'Fnctns' in Figure AII.5, contains the internal functions available in VENSIM which can be copied into the equation as needed. For example, in Figure AII.5 the state variable VOLUME is defined as an INTEG (integer function) drawn from the 'Fnctns' box, of inflows and outflows.

Figure AII.6 illustrates one of the features of VENSIM for constructing a model. The top right button labelled 'Graph Lookup' opens a window where the user can specify actual data inputs which represent the dynamics of a variable, such as precipitation or river flows in a water model, or it can be used to represent a numerical relationship between two variables in the model in a graphical way.

*Figure AII.6 Graphical functions can be entered using the mouse to
actually draw the line, or by entering data values*

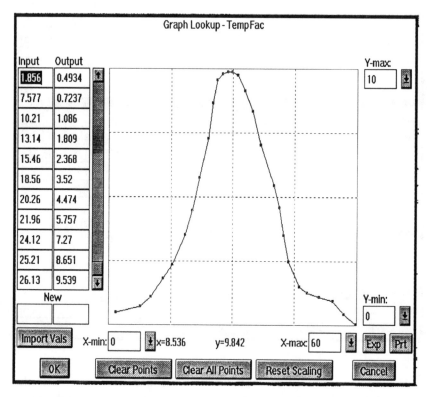

To set the value or enter an equation in a 'constant' , represented by a circle in the model diagram, the user points the cursor to it and double-clicks the mouse button. The equation window pops open, for entering the values and equations in the same way as for the state variable. Running the model is then done with great ease. The user has the choice of defining graphical displays or tables to display results. Options from the 'SIMULATE MODEL' menu-option include the possibility to run sensitivity analysis simulations for specified variables, or to select the integration method to be used in the simulation. All these features make VENSIM a very useful simulation tool for building dynamic systems models, without having to spend so much time in programming and debugging models built with conventional programming languages. In turn this allows the modeller to concentrate on understanding and interpreting the results in terms of the modelling assumptions, which is the most important part of such a learning experience.

AII.4 MODELLING EXAMPLES

AII.4.1 Modelling Population Dynamics

This example is a model of the logistic growth equation. It represents the dynamics of a plant community as an 'S-shaped' curve known as the logistic growth curve, a very commonly used equation in simulating the dynamics of populations which grow exponentially until they reach some maximum level where growth is limited by some density-dependent factor and finally levels off. Here a logistic equation is used to simulate the growth of a plant community. Equation (AII.1) assumes that there is a maximum potential growth that the biomass will attain under ideal conditions. The growth cycle of the plant community is then divided-up into discrete time steps (δt) so as to simulate the process as a continuous dynamic where the growth during any time step t is equal to the sum of the existing biomass at the previous time step plus the growth occurring during the current time step calculated in equation (AII.2).

$$Pop(t) = Pop(t - \delta t) + (\delta x / \delta t) * \delta t \qquad (AII.1)$$
$$\delta x / \delta t = (b - d) * Xt * (1 - Xt / K) \qquad (AII.2)$$

where: $\delta x/\delta t$ = growth in each time step
           b = birth rate
           d = death rate
          Xt = actual growth
          K = carrying capacity

The first step in building the VENSIM model is to create the structural diagram shown in Figure AII.7, using the modelling elements presented in Figure AII.1. A stock or state variable is selected with the pointer, placed in the work-space and a name typed in to label the variable as 'Population'. The flow-line is then selected from the tool-kit at the top margin by clicking once. The pointer is moved into the work-space about three inches from the left side of the Population box, the mouse button is pressed and held down while moving the mouse to stretch the arrow until it touches the population box which is high-lighted as a result. The mouse button is released to complete the operation. To name the flow-line, it is necessary to click on the circle hanging from the flow-line arrow and move the pointer on to the box with text in it until the cursor becomes a thin line, then type in the expression '$\delta x/\delta t$' (ie the change in the variable x over the time period t).

In this example, three 'constants or parameters' (the circles on the tool-kit between the flow-line icon and the arrow) need also to be defined. For each one of the three parameters in Figure AII.7 the parameter icon is clicked once and moved on to the work-space and placed underneath the flow-line arrow on the diagram. They are then named 'Birth', 'Death' and '*pop k*'.

Figure AII.7 VENSIM diagram of the logistic plant model

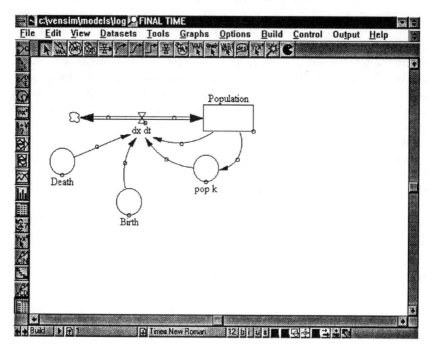

The next step is to connect the parameters to the flow-line valve. The arrow is chosen from the work-space by clicking once over the arrow icon and moving the cursor over a parameter, after which the mouse button is pressed and held down while moving it on to the flow-line valve and releasing the mouse button when the flow-line is highlighted. An additional arrow needs to link the Population box and the *pop k* parameter in the same way as the other arrows were connected. The diagram should now look like the one shown in Figure AII.7.

By clicking twice on the Population box the window for entering the initial value for the population opens to show a screen shown in Figure AII.8. At this time the number '10' is typed and the 'OK' button is clicked to close the window and return to the model diagram. A similar procedure is used to to enter values for the 'birth' and 'death' parameters and finally to portray the the equation for the flow regulator $\delta x/\delta t$.

Figure AII.8 Opening the equation window by clicking in the centre of the box

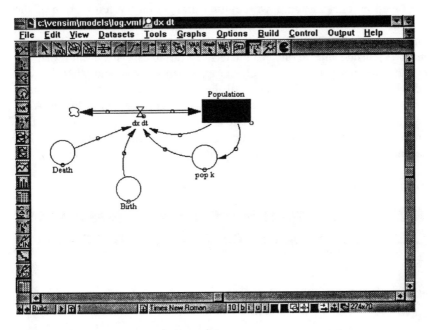

Figure AII.9 Graphical results of the logistic growth model

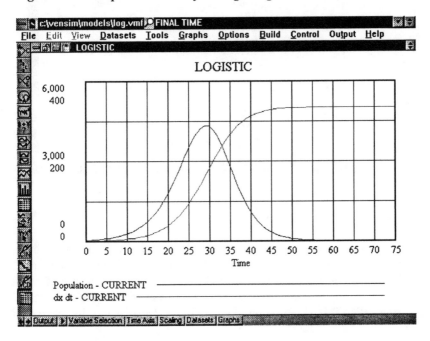

Having completed entering the values and equations which define the model one can examine all the entries in the 'Equations' screen which is displayed by clicking the down-pointing triangle on the left margin of the screen. To proceed, the upward-pointing triangle on the left margin is clicked to return to the model diagram. Sometimes there remains a question-mark (?) inside one of the parameters or variables. This means that the operator has not yet entered a value or an equation for it, and VENSIM will not allow the the model to run until the all the equations and values have been entered. A graphical output for the model is presented in Figure AII.9 and the corresponding table output is shown in Figure AII.10. The first curve in Figure AII.9 is the typical S-shaped logistic growth curve. The second curve is a plot of the change in the population at each time step.

Figure AII.10Table output of the logistic growth model

Time	Population	Runs:	Population	dx dt	Runs:	dx dt
0		CURRENT	10		CURRENT	2.29
1			12.29			2.82
2			15.11			3.46
3			18.58			4.25
4			22.84			5.22
5			28.07			6.41
6			34.49			7.87
7			42.36			9.66
8			52.03			11.84
9			63.87			14.50
10			78.37			17.74
11			96.11			21.68
12			117.80			26.45
13			144.25			32.22
14			176.47			39.15
15			215.63			47.45
16			263.09			57.32
17			320.42			68.97
18			389.39			82.58
19			471.98			98.30

AII.4.2   Reservoir Dynamics

A second example often used to illustrate the dynamics of a system over time is that of a sink or reservoir which has water coming into it and water draining out at the same time. In VENSIM this system is represented graphically in Figure AII.11 as a stock (state variable) named VOLUME, a flow-line called IN, which represents the flows of water into the reservoir;

and another flow-line called OUTFLOW for modelling the flow of water out of the system. At each time step a certain amount of water may flow in, and at the same time water flows out. The water level remaining in the reservoir is the balance of the initial amount of water in the reservoir plus the inflow minus the outflow.When the model is run, VENSIM calculates all these values at each time step (daily or weekly). The user can then define graphical results windows, or tables showing the dynamics of the system over the length of the simulation time in ways that correspond to the discussion outlined above.

Figure AII.11 A VENSIM diagram of a reservoir system

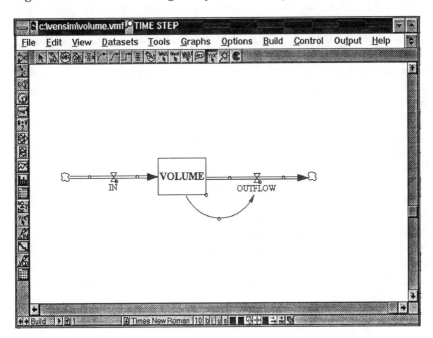

AII.5   SOME GENERAL CONCLUSIONS

A major advantage of VENSIM is the friendliness of the system for developing and running dynamic models. The ease of modelling resides in the interaction between the user and the different alternatives of output representation such as diagrams, graphs and tables. The model can be built and debugged in a fraction of the time it would take to develop an analogous model using traditional programming languages such as FORTRAN, or even simulation languages such as DYNAMO. And once it is built the simulation run can be stopped, examined, and easily modified at any point in time. In this way the user can quickly complete the tasks of debugging and calibrating the model and spend more time learning from the modelling exercise as a whole.

A related advantage is a capacity to check for inconsistencies in model formulation to verify that the user has given an initial value for all the parameters and variables that have been defined in the system before the model can actually run. During this internal checking the model also finds any inconsistencies in its structure which can then be solved by the user. The built-in functions in VENSIM provide a helpful library with pre-set parameters to guide the user in defining equations in the system. These include statistical, trigonometric, economic and simulation functions. Moreover the different window representations allow the user to view the equations, the diagram of system representation and output, in graphs or tables, which facilitate the model evaluation and calibration process. Finally VENSIM requires and promotes interdisciplinary thought. In so doing it helps the analyst to see complicated relationships easily, and if properly used can be of great value for understanding the underlying processes which drive the dynamics of the systems under review.

On the other hand it must also be pointed out that although as a simulation tool VENSIM greatly simplifies the task of building the complex mathematical relationships in a model, this capability is limited. Another limitation is that if the model requires advanced integral functions or partial differential equations to be included to simulate a specific physical processes, it is necessary for these to be computed in another program and then entered manually into VENSIM. Consequently, any modification in the data used to develop any specific function would require the user to manually change these inputs. Overall, however, we would argue that modelling environments, like that of VENSIM, have an important contribution to make in the planning, monitoring and control of complex evolutionary systems.

NOTES

1   See for example the causal-loop diagram as shown in Figure 38, p. 34.

References

Allbaugh, L.G. (1953), *Crete: A Case Study of an Underdeveloped Area*, Princeton, NJ: Princeton University Press.

Altshuler et al. (eds) (1984), *The Future of the Automobile*, Cambridge, Mass.: MIT Press.

Allen P. (1975), 'Darwinian Evolution and Predator-Prey Ecology', *Bulletin of Mathematical Ecology*, **37**, pp. 389–405.

Allen, P.M. (1982), 'The Genesis of Structure in Social Systems', in C. Renfrew et al. (eds), *Theory and Explanation in Archaeology*, London: Academic Press.

Allen, P.M. (1988), 'Why the Whole is Greater than the Sum of the Parts', in W. Woolfe et al. (eds), *Ecodynamics; Contributions to Theoretical Ecology*, Berlin: Springer Verlag.

Allen, P.M. (1989), 'Modelling Innovation and Change' in S.E. van der Leeuw and R. Torrance (eds), *What's New: a Closer look at the Process of Innovation*, London: Unwin Hyman.

Allen, P.M., N.G. Clark and F. Perez-Trejo (1992), 'Strategic Planning of Complex Economic Systems', *Review of Political Economy*, **4** (3), pp. 275–90.

Allen, P.M. and J.M. McGlade (1986), 'Dynamics of Discovery and Exploitation: the Case of the Scotian Shelf Fisheries', *Canadian Journal of Fisheries and Aquatic Sciences*, **43** (6).

Allen, P.M. and J.M. McGlade (1987a), 'Evolutionary Drive: The Effect of Microscopic Diversity, Error making and Noise', *Foundations of Physics*, **17** (7), July, pp. 723–8.

Allen, P.M. and J.M. McGlade (1987b), 'Modelling Complex Human Systems: A Fisheries Example', *European Journal of Operations Research*, **30**, pp. 147–67.

Allen, P.M. and H.K. Phang (1993), 'Evolution, Creativity and Intelligence in Complex Systems', in E. Michailov (eds), *Interdisciplinary Approaches to Complex Systems*, Berlin: Springer Verlag, Synergetics Series.

Allen, P. and M. Sanglier (1979), 'Dynamic Model of Growth in a Central Place System', *Geographical Analysis*, **11**, pp. 256–72.

Allen, P. and M. Sanglier (1981), 'Urban Evolution, Self-Organisation and Decision-Making', *Environment and Planning*, **A21**, pp. 167–83.

Barbier, E.B. (1989), *Economics, Natural-Resource Scarcity and Development*, London: Earthscan.

Barnes, B. (1982), 'The Science–Technology Relationship: a Model and a Query', *Social Studies of Science,* **12,** pp. 166–72.

Beach, E.F. (1957), *Economic Models,* New York: J. Wiley & Sons.

Bell, R.M. and K.L.R. Pavitt (1993), 'Technological Accumulation and Industrial Growth: Contrasts between Developed and Developing Countries', *Industrial and Corporate Change,* **2** (2), pp. 157–210.

Bessant, J. (1990), *Managing Advanced Technology,* Manchester/Oxford: NCC/ Blackwell.

Biggs, S.D. (1974), 'Lament for Policy Oriented Research: Observations on a Research Project to Formulate a Computer Model for Regional Rural Planning in the Kosi Region, Bihar, India', *IDS Bulletin,* **5** (4), pp. 28–36.

Biggs, S.D. (1989), 'Resource poor farmer participation in research: A synthesis of experiences from nine national agricultural research systems', *On-Farm Client-Orientated Research – Comparative study paper no. 3,* The Hague, Netherlands: ISNAR.

Biggs, S.D. (1990), 'A multiple source of innovation model of agricultural research and technology promotion', *World Development,* **18** (11), pp. 1481–99.

Biggs, S. and J. Farrington (1991), *Agricultural Research and the Rural Poor: A Review of Social Science Analysis,* Canada: IDRC.

Biggs, S.D. and J.E. Sumberg (1994), 'Rural Mechanisation and Collegiate Engineering: Policy, Stakeholders and the Search for Common Ground', paper prepared for a workshop on 'Technology for Rural Livelihoods', 6–7 September, Chatham, Kent: NRI.

Biswas, A.K. and S.B.C. Agarwal (eds) (1992), *Environmental Impact Assessment for Developing Countries,* Oxford: Butterworth–Heinemann.

Blue Plan (1992), *Statistics on Population and Economic Activity for the Mediterranean,* Sophia Antipolis,Valbonne, France: Blue Plan Regional Activity Centre.

Boumans, R. and F.H. Sklar (1990), 'A polygon-based spatial (PBS) model for simulating landscape change', *Landscape Ecology,* **4** (2–3).

Cawson, A. (1985), *Organised Interests and the State,* London: Sage Publications.

Cawson, A. (1986), *Corporatism and Political Theory,* Oxford: Basil Blackwell.

CGIAR/TAC (1993), *The Ecoregional Approach to Research in the CGIAR,* FAO (UN), March.

Chambers, R. (1994), 'All Power Deceives', in S. Davies (ed.) (1994), 'Knowledge is Power: The Use and Abuse of Information in Development', *IDS Bulletin,* **25** (2), April.

Chania Statistical Office (1992), *Demographic and Economics Statistics for the Nomos of Chania,* Chania, Greece.

Chapman, M. (1991), 'Building Consensus on Environmental Policy: a New Approach', *Policy Studies,* **12** (4), pp. 20–29.

Chaudhuri, P. (1989), *The Economic Theory of Growth,* London: Harvester/ Wheatsheaf.

Checkland, P. (1981), *Systems Thinking, Systems Practice,* Chichester: John Wiley.

Checkland, P. and J. Scholes (1990), *Soft Systems Methodology in Action,* Chichester: John Wiley.

Cincotta, R. and F. Perez-Trejo (1990), 'A Risk Analysis Methodology for Assessing Natural Resources degradation', *Land Degradation and Rehabilitation,* **2**, pp. 192–9.

Clark, N.G. (1985), *The Political Economy of Science and Technology,* Oxford: Blackwell.

Clark, N.G. (1987), 'Similarities and Differences Between Scientific and Technological Paradigms', *Futures,* **19** (1), February.

Clark, N.G. (1988), 'Some New Approaches to Evolutionary Economics', *Journal of Economic Issues,* **XXII** (2), June.

Clark, N.G. (1990a), 'Development Policy, Technology Assessment and the New Technologies', *Futures,* **25**, November, pp. 913–31.

Clark, N.G. (1990b), 'Evolution, Complex Systems and Technological Change', *Review of Political Economy,* **3** (1), March.

Clark, N.G. (1992), 'Organization & Information in the Evolution of Economic Systems', in J.S. Metcalfe and P. Saviotti (eds), *Evolutionary Theories of Economic and Technical Change: Present State and Future Prospects,* London: Harwood Academic Publishers.

Clark, N.G. (1995), 'The Interactive Nature of Knowledge Systems', *Science and Public Policy,* forthcoming December.

Clark, N.G. and C. Juma (1991), *Biotechnology for Sustainable Development,* Nairobi: ACTS Press.

Clark, N.G. and C. Juma (1992), *Long Run Economics,* London: Pinter Publishers.

Clay, E.J. (1981), 'Food Policy Issues in Low Income Countries: an Overview', *World Bank Staff Working Paper No. 473,* Washington DC: World Bank.

Clay, E.J. and B.B. Schaffer (eds) (1984), *Room for Manoeuvre: An Exploration of Public Policy in Agriculture and Rural Development,* London: Heinemann.

Collins, H.M. (1992), *Changing Order: Replication and Induction in Scientific Practice,* Chicago: Chicago University Press.

Coccossis, H.N. (1991), 'Historical Land-Use Changes: Mediterranean Regions of Europe', in F.M. Brouwer, A.J. Thomas and M.J. Chadwick (eds), *Land-Use Changes in Europe,* Dordrecht: Kluwer Academic Publishers, pp.441–61.

Cole H.S.D., C.Freeman, M. Jahoda and K.L.R. Pavitt (eds) (1973), *Thinking about the Future,* London: Chatto & Windus.

Constant, E.W. (1973), 'A Model for Radical Technological Change Applied to the Turbojet Revolution', *Technology and Culture,* **14** (4), October, pp. 553–72.

Constant, E.W. (1980), *The Origins of the Turbojet Revolution,* Baltimore: Johns Hopkins University Press.

Conway, G.R. (1984), *Rural Resource Conflicts in the UK and the Third World – Issues for Research Policy,* London: Imperial College/SPRU, Papers in Science, Technology and Public Policy.

Conway, G.R. (1993), 'Sustainable Agriculture: the Trade-offs with Productivity, Stability and Equitability', in E.B. Barbier (ed.), *Economics and Ecology,* London: Chapman & Hall.

Costanza, R. and T. Maxwell (1991), 'Spatial ecosystem modelling using parallel processor', *Ecological Modelling*.

Davies, S. (ed.) (1994), 'Knowledge is Power: The Use and Abuse of Information in Development', *IDS Bulletin*, **25** (2), April.

Denison, E.F. (1962), *The Sources of Economic Growth in the US and the Alternatives Before Us*, Supp. Paper 13, New York: Committee for Economic Development.

Desai, A. (1993), *My Economic Affair*, New Delhi: John Wiley Eastern Ltd.

Dosi, G. et al. (eds) (1988), *Technical Change and Economic Theory*, London: Pinter.

Edge, D. (1988), *The Social Shaping of Technology*, PICT Working Paper No. 1, University of Edinburgh: Research Centre for Social Sciences.

Eliasson, G. (1991), 'Modelling the Experimentally Organised Economy', *Journal of Economic Behaviour and Organisation*, **16** (1/2), July, pp. 153–82.

Emery, F.E. (ed.) (1970), *Systems Thinking*, Harmondsworth: Penguin.

Emery, F.E. (1993), 'Policy: Appearance and Reality', in K.B. De Greene (ed.), *A Systems-Based Approach to Policymaking*, Boston: Kluwer Academic Publishers.

Encel, S., P.K. Marstrand and W. Page (1975), *The Art of Anticipation*, London: Martin Robertson.

Engelen, G., R. White and I. Uljee (1993), 'Exploratory Modelling of Socio-Economic Impacts of Climate Change', in G.A. Maul (ed.), *Climate Change in the Intra-American Sea*, London: Arnold, pp. 306–24.

Fagerberg, J. (1995), 'Technology and International Differences in Growth Rates', *Journal of Economic Literature*, forthcoming.

Forrester, J.W. (1968), *Principles of System*, Cambridge, Mass.: MIT Press.

Forrester, J. (1971), *World Dynamics*, Cambridge: Wright-Allen Press.

Fransman, M. (1995), *NTT and the Evolution of the Japanese Information and Communications Industry*, Oxford: Oxford University Press, forthcoming.

Freeman, C. (1974), *The Economics of Industrial Innovation*, Harmondsworth: Penguin, also London: Pinter, 1982 considerably revised.

Freeman, C. (1987), *Technology Policy and Economic Performance: Lessons from Japan*, London: Pinter.

Freeman, C. (1991), 'Japan: a New National Sysytem of Innovation', in G. Eliasson, 'Modelling the Experimentally Organized Economy', *Journal of Economic Behavior and Organization*, **16** (1–2) July, pp.153–82.

Freeman, G.P. (1985), 'National Styles and Policy Sectors: Explaining Structured Variation' *Journal of Public Policy*, **5**, pp. 467–96.

Furtado, C. (1971), *Development and Underdevelopment*, Berkeley: California University Press.

Gardiner, P. and R. Rothwell (1985), 'Tough Customers; Good Designs', *Design Studies*, **6** (1), pp. 7–17.

Gass, G.M. and S.D. Biggs (1993), 'Rural Mechanisation: a Review of Processes, Policies, Practice and Literature', *Project Appraisal*, **8** (3), pp. 157–187.

Gell-Mann, M. (1994), *The Quark and the Jaguar*, New York: Little, Brown & Co.

George, D.A.R. (1988), *Mathematical Modelling for Economists,* London: Macmillan.

Gibbons, M. (ed.) (1994), *The New Production of Knowledge,* London: Sage.

Graves, A.P. (1991), 'Globalisation of the Automobile Industry: The Challenge for Europe' in C. Freeman et al. (eds), *Technology and the Future Of Europe,* London: Pinter Publishers.

Gremmen, B. (1993), 'The Mystery of the Practical Use of Scientific Knowledge', PhD Thesis, Wageningen Agricultural University, The Netherlands.

Grenon, M. and M. Batisse (1989), *Futures for the Mediterranean Basin: The Blue Plan,* Oxford: Oxford University Press.

Gruber, W. and G. Marquis (eds) (1969), *Factors in the Transfer of Technology,* Cambridge, Mass.: MIT Press.

Hardin, G. (1968), 'The Tragedy of the Commons', *Science,* **162,** pp. 1243–8.

Hardin, G. and J. Baden (1977), *Managing the Commons,* San Francisco: W.H. Freeman & Co.

Harrod, R.F. (1939), 'An Essay in Dynamic Theory', *Economic Journal,* **49,** pp. 14–33.

Helldèn, U. (1991), 'Desertification – Time for an assessment?', *Ambio,* **20,** pp. 372–83.

Hicks, D. (1995), 'Publishing, Reputation Building and Corporate Management of the Public/Private Character of Knowledge', *Industry and Corporate Change,* forthcoming.

Hirsch, R.M. (1978), 'Risk Analyses for a Western Supply System: Occoquan Reservoir, *Hydrologic Sciences – Bulletin des Sciences Hydrologiques,* **23** (4), USA, Virginia: Fairfax and Prince William Countries, pp. 475–505.

Hobday, M. (1994a), 'Export-Led Technology Development in the Four Dragons: The Case of Electronics', *Development and Change,* **25** (2), April.

Hobday, M. (1994b), 'Technological Learning in Singapore: a Test Case of Leapfrogging', *Journal of Development Studies,* April.

Hodgson, G. (1993), *Economics and Evolution,* London: Polity Press.

Hoffman, K. and R. Kaplinsky (1988), *Driving Force: the Global Restructuring of Technology, Labour and Investment in the Automobile and Components Industries,* Boulder, Colorado: Westview Press.

Holling, C.S. (1973), 'Resilience and Stability of Ecological Systems', *Annual Review of Ecological Systematics,* **4,** pp. 1–23.

Holling, C.S. (1985), 'Perceiving and Managing the Complexity of Ecological Systems', in *The Science and Praxis of Complexity,* Tokyo: United Nations University.

Humphrey, J. (1995), 'Industrial Reorganisation in Developing Countries: from Models to Trajectories', *World Development,* forthcoming.

Hunt, D. (1989), *Economic Theories of Underdevelopment,* London: Harvester/Wheatsheaf.

IERC (1991), *An Integrated Strategic Planning and Policy Framework for Senegal,* EC Final Report, Article 8 946/89, Cranfield University, UK: IERC, October.

Imai, M. (1986), *Kaizen: The Key to Japan's Competitive Success*, New York: McGraw-Hill.

Imeson, A.C. (1984), 'An eco-geomorphological approach to the soil degradation and erosion problem', in R. Fantechi and N.S. Margaris (eds), *Desertification in Europe: Proceedings of the Information Symposium in the EEC Programme on Climatology*, The Netherlands, Dordrecht: Reidel Publishing Company.

Imeson A.C. and F. Perez-Trejo (1995), 'Desertification Response Units: a spatial dynamic methodology for assessing land degradation in Mediterranean landscapes', in J.B. Thornes,. and J. Brandt (eds), *Mediterranean Desertification and Land Use*, Chichester: John Wiley & Sons, forthcoming.

Jessop, B., K. Bonnett, S. Bromy and T. Ling (1988), 'Popular Capitalism, Flexible Accumulation and Left Strategy', *New Left Review*, no. 165, pp. 104–24.

Jiggins, J.L.S. and H. de Zeeuw (1992), 'Participatory Technology Development in Practice: Process and Methods', in C. Reijntjes, B. Haverkort and A. Waters-Bayer (eds), *Farming for the Future: an Introduction to Low External Input Agriculture*, London: Macmillan and Leusden, ILEIA, pp. 135–62.

Juma, C. (1989), *The Gene Hunters: Biotechnology and the Scramble for Seeds*, Princeton, NJ, Princeton University Press.

Juma, C. and V. Cable (1992), *Shaping our Common Future*, Report prepared for the Centre for Our Common Future, Geneva.

Kaplinsky, R. (1994), *Easternisation: the Spread of Japanese Management Techniques to LDCs*, London: Frank Cass.

Kaplinsky, R. (1995), 'Technique and System: the Spread of Japanese Management Techniquesto Developing Countries', *World Development*, forthcoming.

Kazaklis, A., F. Perez-Trejo and V. Kazana (1992), 'A spatial methodology for assessing the effects of land-use changes in terms of land degradation and desertification', mimeo, IERC, Cranfield Institute of Technology, UK.

Kean, S.A. (1994), 'The Institutional Politics of Agricultural Research Policy in Zambia: a Model of Contingent Innovation', PhD Thesis, School of Development Studies, University of East Anglia, January.

Kinsey, B.H. and I. Ahmed (1983), 'Mechanical Innovations on Small African Farms: Problems of Development and Diffusion', *International Labour Review*, **122** (3).

Kiriro, A. and C. Juma (1991), *Gaining Ground*, Nairobi: ACTS Press.

Klaassen, L. and T.H. Botterweg (1976), 'Project Evaluation and Intangible Effects: a Shadow Project Approach', in P. Nijkamp (ed.), *Environmental Economics*, **1**, Leiden: Martinus Nijhoff.

Kline, S.J. (1985), 'Innovation is not a Linear Process', *Research Management*, July/August, pp. 36–45.

Koestler, A. (1970), *The Ghost in the Machine*, London: Pan Books.

Koestler, A. (1982), *Bricks to Babel*, London: Picador.

Kolodny, E.Y. (1974), *La Population des Isles de la Grèce*, Vol. 1, France: EDISUD, CNRS.

Kuznets, S. (1959), *Economic Growth*, London: Frank Cass.

Kuzucuoglu, C. (1989), *Fires in the Mediterranean Region,* in Blue Plan (1992).

Lee, N. (ed.) (1992), 'Special Issue on Strategic Environmental Assessment', *Project Appraisal,* **7** (3), September.

Leloup, F. (1993), 'Migration Dynamics: A Policy Exploration Tool for Senegal', Ph.D. Thesis, International Ecotechnology Research Centre, Cranfield University, UK.

Leeuwis, C. (1993), 'Of Computers, Myths and Modelling: The Social Construction of Diversity, Knowledge, Information and Communication Technologies in Dutch Agriculture and Agricultural Extension', Doctoral Dissertation, Wageningen Agricultural University, Wageningen, The Netherlands.

Lewis, W.A.(1963), 'Economic Development with Unlimited Supplies of Labour', in A. Agarwal and S. Singh (eds), *The Economics of Underdevelopment,* Oxford: Oxford University Press.

Lindblom, C.E. (1959), 'The Science of "Muddling Through"', *Public Administration Review,* **2**, Spring, pp. 79–88.

Long, N. and A. Long (eds) (1992), *Battlefields of Knowledge,* London: Routledge.

Majone, G. (1980), 'Policies as Theories', *Omega,* **8**.

Malecki, E. J. (1991), *Technology and Economic Development,* Harlow: Longmans.

Mayer, L. (1992), 'Some comments on equilibrium concepts and geomorphic systems', *Geomorphology,* **5**, pp. 277–95.

Meadows, D.H., D.L. Meadows, J. Randers and W.W. Behrens III (1972), *The Limits to Growth,* New York: Potomac Books.

Miller, R., M. Hobday, T. Leroux-Demers and X. Olleros (1995), 'Innovation in Complex Systems: the Case of Flight Simulation', *Industrial and Corporate Change,* forthcoming.

Mitch, W.J., J.K. Cronk and R.M. Sykes (1990), 'Effective modelling of a major inland oil spill on the Ohio river', *Ecological Modelling,* **51**.

Morrison, T.K. (1984), 'Cereal Imports by Developing Countries: Trends and Determinants', *Food Policy,* **9**, pp. 13–26.

Mosley, P. (1984), *The Making of Economic Policy,* Brighton: Wheatsheaf.

Myrdal, G. (1957), *Economic Theory and Underdeveloped Regions,* London: Duckworth.

Mytelka, L.K. (1989), 'The Unfulfilled Promise of African industrialisation', *African Studies Review,* **32** (3), pp. 77–137.

Norgaard, R. (1985), 'Environmental Economics: an Evolutionary Critique and a Plea for Pluralism', *Journal of Environmental Economics and Management,* **12** (4).

NOS (1984), Results of the Census of the Population and Inhabitants, *Social and Demographic Characteristics of the Population,* **2**, Athens: National Office of Statistics, 5 April.

Ormerod, P. and M. Campbell (1993), 'Macroeconomic Modelling of Complex Systems', *Neural Network World,* **6**, pp. 795–814.

Ostrom, E. (1990), *Governing the Commons,* Cambridge: Cambridge University

Press.

Ostrom, E., L. Schroeder and S. Wynne (1993), *Institutional Incentives and Sustainable Development; Infrastructure Policies in Perspective*, Oxford: Westview Press.

Pearce, D., E.B. Barbier and A. Markandya (1992), *Sustainable Development, Economics and Environment in the Third World*, Aldershot: Elgar.

Pearce, D., A. Markandya and E.B. Barbier (1989), *Blueprint for a Green Economy*, London: Earthscan.

Pereira-Mendes, V. (1991), 'R&D Technical Change and Intangible Investment', MPhil. Thesis, SPRU, University of Sussex, UK.

Perez-Trejo, F. (1989), 'Impact Assessment Methodologies for Complex Natural Systems', in P.M. van der Stall and F.A. van Vught (eds), *Impact Forecasting and Assessment: Methods, Results, Experiences*, Delft: Delft University Press.

Perez-Trejo, F. (1995), 'A Model of the dynamics of aggregation in structured soils', in *Models in geobiophysical processes*, CATENA Verlag, forthcoming.

Perez-Trejo, F., N.G. Clark and P.M. Allen (1993a), 'An Exploration of Dynamical Systems Modelling as a Decision Tool for Environmental Policy', *Journal of Environmental Management*, **39**, pp. 101–15.

Perez-Trejo, F., N.G. Clark and V. Kazana (1993b), 'A Dynamic Framework for Exploring Linkages between the Environment, Tourism and Agriculture: A Crete Case Study', mimeo, IERC, Cranfield University. UK.

Perez-Trejo, F. and A. Saez (1995), *The UNEP/UNITAR Training Manual on Environmental Decision-making for Sustainable Development*, Geneva.

Piore, M. and C. Sabel (1984), *The Second Industrial Divide*, New York: Basic Books.

Pollak, S. (1995), 'Computers, Telecommunications and the Microbiologist: The Online Hunt for Microbes', DPhil. Thesis, Science Policy Research Unit, University of Sussex, Brighton, UK.

Quade, E.S. (1989), *Analysis for Public Decisions*, New York: North Holland, rev. edn by G. M. Carter.

Ranis, G. and Fei, G. (1961), 'A Theory of Economic Development', **AER, LI** (4), September.

Redclift, M. (1987), *Sustainable Development*, London: Methuen.

Reid, W. et al. (1993), *Biodiversity Prospecting: Using Genetic Resources for Sustainable Development*, Washington DC: World Resources Institute (WRI).

Richmond, B. (1985), ' STELLA: Software for bringing system dynamics to the other 98%', proceedings of the International Conference of the System Dynamics Society, 2–5 July, Keystone, Colorado, USA.

Ridley, M. (1985), *The Problems of Evolution*, Oxford: Oxford University Press.

Ring, S. and F.H. Sklar (1989), 'Simulating the long-term impacts of coastal development and landscape changes on the ecology of the Waccamaw river, South Carolina', in Magoon et al. (eds), *Proceedings of the Coastal Zone '89 Conference, Sixth Symposium on Coastal and Ocean Management*, Vol. 5.

Röling, N. (1994), 'Communication Support for Sustainable Natural Resource Management', in S. Davies (ed.) (1994), 'Knowledge is Power: The Use and Abuse of Information in Development', *IDS Bulletin*, **25** (2), April.

Rose, R. (1991), 'Comparing Forms of Comparative Analysis', *Political Studies,* **39**, pp. 446–62.

Rosen, R. (1974), 'Planning, Management, Policies and Strategies', *International Journal of General Systems,* **1**.

Rosen, R. (1987), 'On Complex Systems', *European Journal of Operational Research,* **30**.

Rosenberg, N. (1976), *Perspectives on Technology,* Cambridge: Cambridge University Press.

Sanchez, V. and C. Juma (eds) (1994), *Biodiplomacy: Genetic Resources and International Relations,* Nairobi: ACTS Press.

Schmitz, H. (1989), 'Flexible Specialisation: a New Paradigm of Small Scale Industrialisation', Brighton, IDS, University of Sussex.

Schumpeter, J. (1934), *The Theory of Economic Development,* Cambridge: Cambridge University Press.

Schutzelaars, A., G. Engelen, I. Uljee and S. Wargnias (1994), 'Computer Systems That Enhance the Productivity of Public Sector Planners', *International Journal of Public Administration,* **17** (1), pp. 119–54.

Sen, A. (ed.) (1971), *Growth Economics,* Harmondsworth: Penguin.

Sengenberger, W. and F. Pyke (1991), 'Small Firms, Industrial Districts and Local Economic Regeneration', *Labour and Society,* **16** (1), pp. 1–25.

Sklar, F.H. and R. Costanza (1991), 'The development of dynamic spatial models for landscape ecology: a review and prognosis', in M.G. Turner and R.H. Gardner (eds), *Quantitative Methods in Landscape Ecology,* New York: Springer-Verlag.

Soete, L. (1986), 'Technological Innovation and Long Waves', in R. MacLeod (ed.), *Technology and the Human Prospect,* London: Pinter Publishers.

Stein, H. (1992), 'Deindustrialisation,Adjustment, the World Bank and the IMF in Africa', *World Development,* **20** (1), pp. 83–95.

Stirling, A. (1994), 'Diversity and Ignorance in Electricity Supply Investment', *Energy Policy,* **22** (3), March, pp. 195–216.

Sweezy, P.M. (1942), *Theory of Capitalist Development,* New York.

Thomas, J.W. and M.S. Grindle (1990), 'After the Decision: Implementing Policy Reforms in Developing Countries', *World Development,* **18** (8), pp. 1163–81.

Thompson, M. (1993), 'Good Science for Public Policy', *Journal of International Development,* **5** (6), pp. 669–79.

van de Fliert, E. (1993), 'Integrated Pest Management. Farmer Field Schools Generate Sustainable Practices: A Case Study in Central Java Evaluating IPM Training', **WU Papers 93–3**, Wageningen Agricultural University, Wageningen, The Netherlands.

Van Pelt, M.J.F. (1993), 'Ecologically Sustainable Development and Project Appraisal in Developing Countries', *Ecological Economics,* **7**, pp. 19–42.

von Bertalanffy, L. (1950), 'The Theory of Open Systems in Physics and Biology', *Science,* **111**, pp. 23–9.

Waldrop, M.M. (1993), *Complexity,* London: Penguin.

Wallis, K.F. (ed.) (1987), *Models of the UK Economy,* New York: Oxford University Press.

Weigand, C.J. (1986), 'An advanced modelling program: STELLA', *The MACazine*, May.

White, R. and G. Engelen (1993), 'Cellular Automata and Fractal Urban Form: a Cellular Modelling Approach to the Evolution of Urban Land-Use Patterns', *Environment and Planning*, **25**, pp. 1175–99.

Whyte, A.V. and I. Burton (eds) (1980), *Environmental Risk Assessment (Scope Is)*, I.C.S.U., New York: John Wiley & Sons.

Womak, J.P., D.T. Jones and D. Roos (1990), *The Machine that Changed the World*, New York: Macmillan.

World Commission on Environment and Development (1987), *Our Common Future*, Oxford: Oxford University Press.

World Resources Institute (WRI), UNEP, IUCN (1992), *Global Biodiversity Strategy*, Washington DC: WRI.

Wu, J. and J.L. Vankat (1992), 'An area-based model of species richness dynamics', *Ecological Modelling*.

Index

167